Coming Apocalypse

Vernon Coleman

Vernon Coleman: What the papers say

'Vernon Coleman writes brilliant books.' – *The Good Book Guide*
'No thinking person can ignore him.' – *The Ecologist*
'The calmest voice of reason.' – *The Observer*
'A godsend.' – *Daily Telegraph*
'Superstar.' – *Independent on Sunday*
'Brilliant!' – *The People*
'Compulsive reading.' – *The Guardian*
'His message is important.' – *The Economist*
'He's the Lone Ranger, Robin Hood and the Equalizer rolled into one.' – *Glasgow Evening Times*
'The man is a national treasure.' – *What Doctors Don't Tell You*
'His advice is optimistic and enthusiastic.' – *British Medical Journal*
'Revered guru of medicine.' – *Nursing Times*
'Gentle, kind and caring' – *Western Daily Press*
'His trademark is that he doesn't mince words. Far funnier than the usual tone of soupy piety you get from his colleagues.' – *The Guardian*
'Dr Coleman is one of our most enlightened, trenchant and sensitive dispensers of medical advice.' – *The Observer*
'I would much rather spend an evening in his company than be trapped for five minutes in a radio commentary box with Mr Geoffrey Boycott.' – Peter Tinniswood, *Punch*
'Hard hitting...inimitably forthright.' – *Hull Daily Mail*
'Refreshingly forthright.' – *Liverpool Daily Post*
'Outspoken and alert.' – *Sunday Express*
'Dr Coleman made me think again.' – *BBC World Service*
'Marvellously succinct, refreshingly sensible.' – *The Spectator*
'Probably one of the most brilliant men alive today.' – *Irish Times*
'King of the media docs.' – *The Independent*
'Britain's leading medical author.' – *The Star*
'Britain's leading health care campaigner.' – *The Sun*
'Perhaps the best known health writer for the general public in the world today.' – *The Therapist*
'The patient's champion.' – *Birmingham Post*

Books by Vernon Coleman include:

Medical
The Medicine Men
Paper Doctors
Everything You Want To Know About Ageing
The Home Pharmacy
Aspirin or Ambulance
Face Values
Stress and Your Stomach
A Guide to Child Health
Guilt
The Good Medicine Guide
An A to Z of Women's Problems
Bodypower
Bodysense
Taking Care of Your Skin
Life without Tranquillisers
High Blood Pressure
Diabetes
Arthritis
Eczema and Dermatitis
The Story of Medicine
Natural Pain Control
Mindpower
Addicts and Addictions
Dr Vernon Coleman's Guide to Alternative Medicine
Stress Management Techniques
Overcoming Stress
The Health Scandal
The 20 Minute Health Check
Sex for Everyone
Mind over Body
Eat Green Lose Weight
Why Doctors Do More Harm Than Good
The Drugs Myth

Complete Guide to Sex
How to Conquer Backache
How to Conquer Pain
Betrayal of Trust
Know Your Drugs
Food for Thought
The Traditional Home Doctor
Relief from IBS
The Parent's Handbook
Men in Bras, Panties and Dresses
Power over Cancer
How to Conquer Arthritis
How to Stop Your Doctor Killing You
Superbody
Stomach Problems – Relief at Last
How to Overcome Guilt
How to Live Longer
Coleman's Laws
Millions of Alzheimer Patients Have Been Misdiagnosed
Climbing Trees at 112
Is Your Health Written in the Stars?
The Kick-Ass A–Z for over 60s
Briefs Encounter
The Benzos Story
Dementia Myth

Psychology/Sociology
Stress Control
How to Overcome Toxic Stress
Know Yourself (1988)
Stress and Relaxation
People Watching
Spiritpower
Toxic Stress
I Hope Your Penis Shrivels Up
Oral Sex: Bad Taste and Hard To Swallow
Other People's Problems

The 100 Sexiest, Craziest, Most Outrageous Agony Column
Questions (and Answers) Of All Time
How to Relax and Overcome Stress
Too Sexy To Print
Psychiatry
Are You Living With a Psychopath?

Politics and General
England Our England
Rogue Nation
Confronting the Global Bully
Saving England
Why Everything Is Going To Get Worse Before It Gets Better
The Truth They Won't Tell You...About The EU
Living In a Fascist Country
How to Protect & Preserve Your Freedom, Identity & Privacy
Oil Apocalypse
Gordon is a Moron
The OFPIS File
What Happens Next?
Bloodless Revolution
2020
Stuffed
The Shocking History of the EU

Diaries
Diary of a Disgruntled Man
Just another Bloody Year
Bugger off and Leave Me Alone
Return of the Disgruntled Man
Life on the Edge
The Game's Afoot
Tickety Tonk

Animals
Why Animal Experiments Must Stop
Fighting For Animals
Alice and Other Friends

Animal Rights – Human Wrongs
Animal Experiments – Simple Truths

General Non Fiction
How to Publish Your Own Book
How to Make Money While Watching TV
Strange but True
Daily Inspirations
Why Is Public Hair Curly
People Push Bottles Up Peaceniks
Secrets of Paris
Moneypower
101 Things I Have Learned
100 Greatest Englishmen and Englishwomen
Cheese Rolling, Shin Kicking and Ugly Tattoos
One Thing after Another

Novels (General)
Mrs Caldicot's Cabbage War
Mrs Caldicot's Knickerbocker Glory
Mrs Caldicot's Oyster Parade
Mrs Caldicot's Turkish Delight
Deadline
Second Chance
Tunnel
Mr Henry Mulligan
The Truth Kills
Revolt
My Secret Years with Elvis
Balancing the Books
Doctor in Paris
Stories with a Twist in the Tale (short stories)

The Young Country Doctor Series
The Bilbury Chronicles
Bilbury Grange
Bilbury Revels
Bilbury Pie (short stories)

Bilbury Country
Bilbury Village
Bilbury Pudding (short stories)
Bilbury Relish
Bilbury Mixture
Bilbury Delights
Bilbury Joys
Bilbury Tales
Bilbury Days
Bilbury Memories

Novels (Sport)
Thomas Winsden's Cricketing Almanack
Diary of a Cricket Lover
The Village Cricket Tour
The Man Who Inherited a Golf Course
Around the Wicket
Too Many Clubs and Not Enough Balls

Cat books
Alice's Diary
Alice's Adventures
We Love Cats
Cats Own Annual
The Secret Lives of Cats
Cat Basket
The Cataholics' Handbook
Cat Fables
Cat Tales
Catoons from Catland

As Edward Vernon
Practice Makes Perfect
Practise What You Preach
Getting Into Practice
Aphrodisiacs – An Owner's Manual
The Complete Guide to Life

Written with Donna Antoinette Coleman
How to Conquer Health Problems between Ages 50 & 120
Health Secrets Doctors Share With Their Families
Animal Miscellany
England's Glory
Wisdom of Animals

Coming Apocalypse

Vernon Coleman

The Author

Dr Vernon Coleman MB ChB DSc FRSA was the first qualified
medical practitioner to question the significance of the 'crisis' with
which you may be familiar, telling readers of his website
www.vernoncoleman.com at the end of February that he felt that the
team advising the Government had been unduly pessimistic and had
exaggerated the danger of the bug. At the beginning of March, he
explained how and why the mortality figures had been distorted.
And on March 14th he warned that the Government's policies would
result in far more deaths than the disease itself. In a YouTube video
recorded on 18th March, he explained his fear that the Government
would use the 'crisis' to oppress the elderly and to introduce
compulsory inoculation. And he revealed that the infection had been
downgraded on March 19th when the public health bodies in the UK
and the Advisory Committee on Dangerous Pathogens decided that
the 'crisis' infection should no longer be classified as a 'high
consequence infectious disease'. Just days after the significance of
the infection had been officially downgraded, the Government
published an Emergency Bill which gave the police extraordinary
new powers and put millions of people under house arrest. Dr
Coleman, a former GP principal, is a *Sunday Times* bestselling
author. His books have sold over two million copies in the UK, been
translated into 25 languages and sold all around the world. He has
given evidence to the House of Commons and the House of Lords
and his campaigning has changed Government policy. There is a
short biography at the back of this book. His website has recently
become difficult to find on the internet.

VERY IMPORTANT NOTE

This book deals with the decision in the early spring of 2020 to put large populations under house arrest and to close factories, shops and all businesses not regarded as essential. It also deals with the aftermath of those decisions. The part dealing with the lockdowns is based entirely on fact. The part dealing with the future is, inevitably, largely conjecture. In order to publish this book I was informed that I had to remove all references to the name of the problem which triggered the close downs. And so you will not find herein any reference to a word describing a disease which begins with the third letter of the alphabet. Nor will you find any reference to a disease name which ends with a number which is slightly greater than 18 and slightly smaller than 20. In addition, in view of proposed new legislation which will make it illegal for anyone (including doctors) to share facts and opinions about a specific medical procedure, I have avoided using a word beginning with 'v' and used the word inoculation instead.

Dedication

To Antoinette,
God blessed me when he brought us together. Without
you I would be only half a person. With you I am whole.
You give me all my passion and all my purpose and I give
you all my love. We are what used to be called
yokefellows – sharing all burdens.

Preface

Right from the start I told you it was the biggest hoax in history. I felt strongly that it wasn't going to be a rerun of the plague and I believed that the so-called experts had got it wrong and had, for whatever reasons, manufactured a false 'crisis'. Back at the beginning of March, I was right in suggesting that populations were not going to die in the numbers that the mathematicians suggested. I described it as a jumped up little flu infection but suggestions that the 'crisis' infection could be compared to the ordinary flu were officially dismissed as 'dangerous nonsense'.

There was a widespread misconception that the models devised by the mathematicians at Imperial College in London were providing accurate and scientific predictions. In reality, they were offering nothing more than extrapolations – the posh word for estimates – and could in no way be regarded as science.

I was the first to suggest that the so-called 'cure' (the lockdown policies and the refusal to treat other patients to 'protect' them from infection) would kill far more people than the disease. The lockdown policies seem to have been recommended by a panicky World Health Organisation, though Imperial College's prediction of eight million Britons in hospital and half a million deaths certainly helped to spice up the panic in the UK.

My criticisms of the Government's policy were sniffily dismissed with the sanctimonious reminder that lives were at stake. However, back in mid-March, it seemed quite obvious that the exaggerated response to the infection was going to do massive harm to the health of the nation and that far more people were going to die as a result of the 'cure' than would die from the disease.

So now it is time to assess the damage that has been done and see how the 'cure' will damage our way of life and dominate everything we do for decades.

I hope I'm wrong this time because I suspect that the so-called 'cure' will do more damage to the way we live than anything else anyone can remember since the plague swept through Europe.

I'm afraid, however, that I believe I am right again.

The politicians, the scientists, the advisors and the media who all promoted this ill-described 'crisis' as though it were a second coming of the plague, will doubtless all insist that the damage done by the lockdown was necessary. (I prefer the more accurate term 'house arrest' to the rather Orwellian 'lockdown'). They will insist that there will be few long-term consequences from their combined stupidity and betrayal. Indeed, I am pretty confident that they will claim (against all the evidence) that it was only their lockdown policy which saved us from far more deaths. Knighthoods and peerages will no doubt be distributed to those who promoted the idea of a 'crisis' requiring unprecedented treatment. However, I believe that their policies have caused far more deaths than they have prevented. If accurate figures are ever obtained, they will prove me right. (The plight of poorer countries is being ignored. Around the world one billion people rely on the $715 billion sent back home by workers in rich countries. Huge numbers of those people will starve without that money.)

Moreover, the evidence shows that those countries which did not put their citizens under house arrest, have suffered far fewer deaths than those countries which did.

The long-term effect of the most egregiously stupid public policies in history, and the failure of public health management, will be to take many nations back into the Dark Ages. The appallingly designed solution will ensure that countries which have ventured into the absurd lunacy of lockdowns will cause chaos and destroy capitalism in just the way the climate change campaigners were demanding.

I was, I fear, right about the hoax.

Now, in this short book, I will summarise what has happened so far and then explain how I think our lives are going to be affected.

Vernon Coleman, 30th April 2020

Part One

It's already worse, far, far worse than you can imagine.

In just a couple of hectic, panicky months governments around the world (with the exception of Sweden and one or two other countries which have not introduced lockdowns and which as a result now appear to have been able to avoid disruption and an exceptional death rate), have introduced measures which will change forever the lives of their citizens.

Nothing is going to be the same again.

Life will never be as good as it was in January 2020.

In less than three months, many people around the world have gone from living in democracies to living in police states.

I was shocked when I first saw terrified shoppers hurrying round the supermarkets with scarfs or masks over their mouths and gloves on their hands. As they skipped around one another, it reminded me of the dancing mania which was a feature of mainland Europe from the 14th century onwards. I suffer from hay-fever and I was terrified of being unable to suppress a sneeze while shopping. It would have been as big a social faux pas as being presented to the Queen and keeping my hands in my pockets or walking into the pavilion at Lords while wearing a jacket with a zip up the front. I could imagine a Bateman cartoon entitled 'The Man Who Sneezed in the Supermarket during Lockdown'.

Banishing all that fear would take a good deal of work.

But do governments really want to banish the fear which has turned citizens into fearful and obedient zombies?

Moreover, we still don't know when the house arrests will end and when something like 'normal' life will be allowed to restart.

There are calls from some to keep social distancing going until 2022. Even if the lockdown stops there is no guarantee that panicky politicians won't bring it back. Some climate change fanatics and 'green' zealots will doubtless want to keep the lockdown in place for as long as possible – they see it as an excellent opportunity to destroy capitalism, break the structure of modern life and further their own aims. New bugs are constantly being discovered and the media has already shown that it is ready, willing and able to help build a modest scare into a major, full-blooded potential holocaust. We are 'fighting battles' and we are in a 'war'. The language is deliberately designed to discourage dissent.

Politicians are terrified of making decisions that might prove controversial. They are, I suspect, even more fearful of being shown to have over-reacted. Politicians don't like the voters to know that they panicked.

Some of the threats made have been awesomely stupid. In the UK stories about panic buying resulted in threats of rationing – as though that would reduce the panic buying! There have been threats to remove 'exercise privileges' though if this went ahead millions of people would have to live under arrest conditions which would be considered barbaric if those under arrest were real criminals. Even murderers in jail are allowed periods of exercise.

Elderly people who were not even suffering from infectious diseases were forced to die alone, without being allowed to see friends or relatives.

I suspect that churches will lose a good deal of support as a result of closing during the 'crisis'. Most churches and cathedrals could have easily accepted their small congregations without any risk to social distancing legislation. Supermarkets stayed open to provide food for the body and I believe churches should have stayed open to provide spiritual comfort. The 'crisis' was the perfect time for churches to provide support. Depriving people of their spiritual comfort at their time of greatest need must have helped to break down morale. Organised religion has had a very bad 'crisis' and I suspect that many churches will struggle to gather in their flocks again when the 'crisis' is over.

The long-term changes to our way of life will be massive and permanent. And the changes will all be a result of the 'cure' and not the 'problem'. Commentators talk of the 'crisis' causing unemployment and so on but the truth is that the 'crisis' will not cause unemployment – it will be the so-called cure which will cause unemployment.

Are these changes accidental? Or were they deliberately engineered? I find it difficult to believe anything the Government says or does these days.

(I actually found myself wondering whether Boris Johnson had really been as seriously ill as reported in the media, or whether his illness was exaggerated as an excuse to avoid having to take responsibility and make a decision about keeping the nation under house arrest. I make no excuse for this level of paranoia. Under the unusual circumstances I actually think it is inevitable and perfectly healthy.)

It is difficult to avoid the suspicion that the plan was to get rid of independent thinking, to force people to be fearful and obedient and to create poverty (poor people tend to be dependent). There is, after all, absolutely no doubt that the mortality figures mentioned have been massively exaggerated to support the position of governments around the world. It is now pretty clear that when the dust settles, the cause of the terror will be shown to have been no more deadly than a moderate edition of the flu. (I know that the disease is not much like flu in the way it affects the human body. But the talk has all been about numbers and deaths. And in those terms, this disease is not as much of a threat as a fairly bad influenza. And it never has been.)

The mortality figures are distorted, however, because people are being listed as victims even when they simply died with the disease rather than of it. To say someone died with a particular disease is as useful as saying they died with athlete's foot or varicose veins. In truth, I suspect that more people have died with varicose veins than have died with the cause of our global despair. Distorting the truth has enhanced the fear but done nothing to improve our understanding of the disease.

In the UK, there is some evidence that between a third and a half of the nation may have or may have had the infection. Without testing we cannot possibly know. Around 650,000 people die every year in the UK. Is the Government really planning to claim that between a third and a half of all this year's 650,000 deaths will be associated with the disease? That would truly be a deceit of brobdingnagian proportions. The UK Government has made a great deal of the fact that 100 health and care workers have died in the UK since the scare began. It has been suggested that they died 'with' the disease but the cleverly implied but false assumption is always that they died 'of' it. And although it is a tragedy that those people died, no one has pointed out that there are around 1,500,000 people employed in the health and care services in the UK and, sadly, some of them die every year. In fact, the figure of 100 deaths among health service workers is no greater than would normally be expected.

The only thing we know for sure is that the cure for the disease (the lockdown and the social distancing and so on) has caused massive disruption to life. And it is clear that it is the cure which will cause the most dramatic long-term effects. The British Government has admitted that their cure will probably kill 150,000 people and that could easily prove to be an underestimate. No one is now claiming that the disease will kill a fraction of that number. Statistics already show that the number of deaths with other causes has risen dramatically since the lockdown began.

Governments may, of course, have been tempted to deliberately exaggerate the number of deaths in order to try to justify their draconian, totalitarian policies.

I suspect that all countries around the world will eventually realise just how much damage their lockdowns have done.

So, since there can now be no doubt that the cure is going to do far more harm than the disease, the big question is: has it happened accidentally (the cock-up theory) or deliberately (the conspiracy theory)?

I doubt if anyone will ever know.

Politicians and their advisors are never going to admit that they got things badly wrong. And the media has been so wedded to this 'crisis' that they are never going to admit that their headlines were fake – and that the fear they engendered was unnecessary.

And they are certainly never going to admit that there was a conspiracy theory behind what has happened.

But, in a way, it doesn't matter.

We still have to be aware of the problems which now lie ahead. And we have to know how we can deal with them; how we can protect our families and ourselves.

On the pages ahead I have summarised how we got where we are (and shown how it was possible to see that the 'crisis' was fake at a very early stage), detailed my forecasts for the future – and the ways in which we can survive in a world where governments' cures have destroyed our way of life.

But first let's take a look at precisely what happened.

I was the first person to cry 'Hoax' when the scare began.

How did I know?

Well, I've been writing about medical matters for half a century and in that time I have seen many scares come and go. I was the first doctor to spot that the AIDS crisis was being massively exaggerated. I was the first doctor to spot the problem with the over-prescribing of benzodiazepines. I have a long track record of providing accurate forecasts. (There is a list on my website www.vernoncoleman.com – if you can find it – and in my book *How To Stop Your Doctor Killing You*.)

I have learned to spot when the medical establishment, the politicians and the media are exaggerating a danger and missing simple truths.

(I mention these things not to boast but because it seems necessary to establish my credentials – particularly since my stance on this issue means that I have been subjected to much abuse, much disinformation and many plain, old-fashioned lies.)

It doesn't matter whether the fiasco was a result of a conspiracy or a cockup – the bottom line is that we are heading for an apocalypse and we are going to have to trust ourselves and one another because we certainly cannot trust our so-called leaders or their advisors – the people who are pretending to run the world. We cannot trust our leaders because they aren't on our side; they are either desperately stupid and incompetent or they are as crooked as hell and only interested in taking power – and keeping it. In the UK, Prime Minister Boris Johnson and his ministers and all the Government's advisors should resign or be sacked. Naturally, neither will happen. In America, I suspect that Donald Trump has had as good a 'crisis' as any leader. Unless something else happens, he has, I suspect, pretty well ensured that he will be re-elected to the Presidency – whenever the elections take place.

And we cannot trust the media to question what we are being told.

Throughout the 'crisis' the media has been supine – readily repeating what they are told by governments everywhere and never questioning the wisdom of lockdowns, rising police powers and so on. The media has lost all respect and credibility. The 'crisis' has not been their finest hour. On the whole, editors and journalists have shown no courage whatsoever.

And I fear that what has happened in 2020 will happen again in the future.

First because the 'experts' are claiming that mutations will mean that there will be more crises. (If you put a great deal of effort into terrifying populations then you have to keep exerting pressure in order to keep the terror levels high.)

Second because those same experts have said that even people who have been ill and who have therefore acquired immunity to it may still catch the disease a second or a third time. This is very peculiar and I find it difficult to believe but it doesn't matter a damn what you or I believe. All that matters is what the experts and the politicians believe (or find it convenient to believe) because it is what they believe which will define the legislation they introduce and the rules they bring in. And, of course, if you can catch the disease two or three times then you'll need stuff injected into you. (They will no doubt explain, convincingly, that the stuff from inside a syringe can somehow provide a level of immunity far greater than is possible with the disease itself.)

And third because I have no doubt that more diseases will be coming our way. Infections have been a growing problem for some years. The increase in travel by aeroplanes has meant that bugs can travel around the world in a matter of hours. A misplaced reliance on antibiotics has made people careless. And the over-use of antibiotics by farmers and doctors has resulted in the development of many antibiotic resistant infections. Appalling hygiene practises in hospitals has meant the spread of lethal infections within hospitals. And those infections have then been taken out into the community – largely by hospital staff going out while still wearing their hospital uniforms. There is, of course, also the risk created by circumstances in China and other parts of Asia where the consumption of live animals is considered acceptable.

I don't believe that there are necessarily many more infective organisms around these days than there were, say, five or ten years ago but I do believe that the people who manufactured the 2020 lockdowns will be looking for more opportunities to close down nations and to keep people imprisoned in their homes. And our reliance on epidemiologists with doubtful records will lead to unnecessary restrictions.

(It isn't just the epidemiologists who are a threat. Politicians have also taken to offering advice. The mayor of London told commuters to wear masks even though the medical advice was at the time equivocal and the World Health Organisation seemed to rule against them. Everyone is a medical expert these days; propaganda and political expediency have taken over from news. Since there are few masks available for sale, people are being advised to make their own and there are books and articles around explaining to do this. Since masks are single use only – and have to be carefully disposed of after use (preferably incinerated) I am intrigued to know how people will find the time and materials to make several masks a day each. Naturally, the haberdashery shops which would provide the essential materials are all classed as non-essential and, even if they were open, anyone leaving their home to purchase the required materials would risk arrest.)

The consequences of the 'crisis' will be far reaching. We are going to have to pay a huge price. Nothing is ever going to be as it was. It will take generations to escape from the chaos and economic misery caused by this absurdly hysterical overreaction. Indeed, the economic chaos facing us all is so great that, among the wildest conspiracy theories is the notion that the whole fiasco is merely a cover to destroy capitalism and satisfy climate change campaigners.

Governments and advisors have completely destroyed the world we know. I repeat: we are all going to have to pay a massive price for the global lockdowns.

And yet there was never any evidence that lockdowns would help. The evidence shows that they have done far more harm than good. I have seen claims in the press that every country has put its citizens under house arrest but this is not true.

Countries such as South Korea, Singapore, Taiwan, Sweden and Japan which did not put their citizens under house arrest have had fewer deaths than countries which introduced strict restrictions. (It may be, of course, that those countries which introduced hard house-arrest rules have had more deaths because they have been artificially inflating their figures in order to try to justify their aggressive, totalitarian policies.)

On 20th April it was reported that in Sweden the peak of the spread had passed. It isn't much of a flight of fancy to assume that whereas those countries which closed their economies will collapse, those countries, such as Sweden, which did not accept the hysterical approach, will have an incredibly bright future and will prove to be incredibly successful in the coming years.

As an aside, it is significant and relevant that the decisions which have destroyed national and global economies have all been taken by individuals who receive state salaries and who will receive state pensions. They will not be exposed to the costly losses the wider economy will suffer.

We are, I say again, heading for an apocalypse.

The seriously troubling days of lockdowns, road blocks and threats of rationing may have seemed scary but they were the days of relative calm before a manufactured storm of unprecedented ferocity. I suppose the world's governments could have made a bigger mess of dealing with the 'crisis' but it is difficult to see how.

I began making the notes which have turned into this book to help myself decide what Antoinette and I have to do to cope with the new world we are going to have to live in. And then I started to prepare an article for my website. But before I knew what was happening, the notes and the article had grown into a short book.

I am going to describe how the story unfolded and how mistake after mistake made things worse – with the authorities steadily making things worse with everything they did, and creating ever-expanding problems for the future.

You may disagree with some of my conclusions. You may disagree with the way I intend to tackle the problems which lie ahead. Indeed, judging by what has happened in the last month or so I suspect that I'll be subjected to another campaign of lies, libels and disinformation. I'm not sure that I care anymore. But please remember that this is not the first time I've been right and the authorities and medical establishment have been wrong.

Surprisingly, many citizens around the world have welcomed the lockdown restrictions. They will certainly welcome a book which questions the very need for any sort of restrictions.

Even more surprisingly is the fact that the British appear to be the most enthusiastic about the restrictions. One opinion poll showed that 84% of Britons believe that they will face years of economic hardship as a result of the lockdowns (heaven knows what mind-bending drugs the other 16% are taking) but astonishingly 44% think that the restrictions are not severe enough.

I found this particularly surprising since in other countries there has been real opposition to being put under house-arrest. Even the Germans, not usually regarded as rebellious folk, have protested.

More predictably, in the United States, the opposition to widespread house arrest has been determined. In the state of Michigan, the local sheriffs issued a statement saying that they would not help enforce the governor's order to stay at home.

In the UK I have discovered at first hand that those even questioning the Government or its advisors are likely to be subjected to horrendous abuse. My second and third videos on YouTube were hidden in a dark, dingy corner of the internet. My website, which has been prominently displayed for a quarter of a century, has also been banished to a dark corner. I wonder why that could be. And Facebook tells me that the Facebook page they wouldn't let me have ('in order to protect the Facebook community') has now been disabled. This came as something of a surprise since I'm not sure you can disable something that has never been abled. It is, I confess, rather confusing to find Zuckerberg et al trying to claim the high moral ground. It's a bit like imagining Adolf Hitler standing in a pulpit preaching a fire and brimstone sermon.

Hopefully, the ideas on the following pages will help you decide how best to manage your life in order to survive.

Make no mistake: the future is now about survival.

I fear that we are now about to enter the worst and the longest recession in modern history – certainly the worst in living memory.

And I fear that the lockdown which started in the early spring of 2020 will not be the last. It's going to happen again.

If, as some people believe, there has been a conspiracy and we have experienced a false emergency created partly in order to distract us from very real problems in our society and partly to enable politicians around the world to take control of our lives, then we have to understand what is being planned – and we have to make plans of our own. As I pointed out earlier on, we are going to have to trust ourselves and one another because we certainly cannot trust our so-called leaders, or their advisors or the mass media.

If, on the other hand, the 'crisis' fiasco was the result of total incompetence then we still have to deal with the consequences ourselves. We cannot expect our leaders miraculously to acquire the competence required to steer us through the difficulties which lie ahead. And we must expect another similar fiasco not too far in the future. The circumstances which led to the 'crisis' of 2020 are not going away. Nothing has changed. There are plenty of strange infections around, and international air travel means that diseases can spread around the world in a day or two. The chances of our avoiding another scare are nil.

Part Two describes how we got into this mess. I've reproduced, in diary form, my account of the events as they unfolded. (I haven't changed any of this other than to remove the words which originally resulted in this book being refused publication. The essence of these entries appeared on my website.)

And Part Three describes and explains the future I think we now have. The so-called 'cure' for this disease will, as so often happens in medicine, cause far more trouble than the disease itself. Governments almost everywhere have made an endless series of huge miscalculations and have exhibited an inhuman obsession with the disease to the exclusion of everything else.

Part Two

This section of this book is taken from my diary, running from February 2020 to the middle of April 2020 when it appeared increasingly clear to me that the Government's advisors had got their forecasts completely wrong and that what I see as egregious incompetence, combined with a panicky Government struggling through a mist of woolly-minded confusion, had damned near destroyed the country. Readers who followed my articles on my website www.vernoncoleman.com will know that these comments were contemporaneous. My videos on YouTube are, of course, dated so there can be no doubts about those either.

February 28th 2020

As the care continues, the public are being advised to use hand sterilising wipes or fluid and to avoid touching their eyes. According to the World Health Organisation, masks aren't likely to be much help, though they would obviously be useful for anyone intending to rob a bank.

GPs have told patients who think they might be affected to keep away from their surgeries and to telephone 111. Unfortunately, the advice from 111 appears to be to trot along to the local hospital and wait there.

Maybe the authorities aren't handling this quite as well as they should be doing.

And if the Government had been really worried it would, of course, have made far more sense to stop all flights between China and the UK.

Still, that would have been bad for business.

Meanwhile, there is much concern that the Chinese might be suppressing some facts. My own experience with the Chinese makes me worry. A few years ago I wrote a column for a large Chinese newspaper. One week I wrote a piece about inoculation. The result was to ban the column and fire me. Fair enough. But within days my

Chinese book publishers (who had been very successful with a number of my medical books) wrote to tell me that they would no longer be dealing with me. The books they had would no longer be sold and they would not consider any new books. I subsequently wrote to several other Chinese publishers. None of them would have anything to do with my books – even though the previous publisher must have made quite a lot of money out of them. I was told that within days the Chinese Government had introduced a widespread ban on all medical books by foreign authors.

Imagine how the Chinese might act to suppress news about a potentially serious epidemic which would have an effect on their reputation and economy.

As it is I confess I am puzzled by the fuss being made about a disease which appears to be no more than a variation on something which has been around for half a century. The fuss is causing panic everywhere, and the world's stock markets are in free fall as analysts get terribly excited and take advantage of the 'crisis' to suggest that investors sell equities. The American stock market has been overvalued for ages and there are many uncertainties in the world so brokers seem keen to use the threat as an excuse to sell. I don't believe for a second that the fall in share prices is entirely due to a disease that does not yet have a place in the Chamber of Horrors.

Elsewhere, holidaymakers are cancelling trips and shoppers are panic buying. Soap has never been as popular.

Doctors working in the NHS say that the elderly will be sacrificed so that millennials will be able to live.

So, what the devil is going on?

The figures that have been released really do not suggest that this is going to be a new version of the Spanish `flu which affected a third of the world's population and killed at least 20 million in 1918.

But despite the evidence, broadcast and print media seem determined to turn the story into a source of mass panic.

Around the world up to 600,000 people a year die from the common or garden variety of flu, and the new disease is at the moment a much, much smaller threat.

Is there a hidden agenda here?

Maybe the plan is to use the 'crisis' as an excuse to put a stop to unnecessary travel (i.e., any travel not being undertaken by politicians, celebrities, members of the royal family or enthusiastic supporters of climate change mythology). This would enable the authorities to cut down the use of oil, a disappearing commodity, and, therefore, save the stuff so that people like Prince Charles can continue travelling around the world telling the rest of us to stay at home.

Or maybe the aim is to soften us up and prepare us for compulsory inoculation. There will doubtless be stuff from a syringe available within a few months and if the scare is big enough the authorities will be able to introduce laws forcing us all to be inoculated. And once one type of inoculation becomes compulsory then the same will happen with other stuff from syringes.

Am I being paranoid?

No. I don't think so.

March 2nd 2020

I strongly suspect that the mortality figures are distorted because the authorities are only identifying people with severe bouts of the disease. Think of flu: millions of people get flu but never report their symptoms to a doctor. They know there is little point. But the authorities seem to be wrongly assuming that the mortality rate can be ascertained by measuring the number of deaths against the number of patients seen by doctors. (If 1,000 people go to their doctor with the flu, and 1 of those patients dies, then the mortality rate is 0.1%. But if another 9,000 people have the flu but don't go to their doctors, then the mortality rate is 0.01%.)

March 3rd 2020

The hysteria grows and the more the hysteria grows the more the confusion grows. I am still harbouring a suspicion that the whole exercise could be to exclude the elderly from health care – and, indeed, from society. Maybe the Government wants to get rid of old people so that it won't have to keep paying out pensions.

The WHO now agrees with me that currency could spread the disease. Why did it take so long? Will governments and central banks use the 'crisis' as an excuse to create a cashless society? It's what they desperately want and so I can see it happening. The fact is that the risk from currency is no greater than the risk of picking up the disease from all sorts of other things that people handle – door knobs, for example.

People are so terrified that many are behaving in odd ways. I've seen pictures of people wearing plastic boxes on their heads. This is pretty pointless. If you can still breathe then the air is getting into your plastic box. And the air will contain the bugs you are trying to avoid. I suppose the box might help prevent you being infected if someone coughed straight at you. The fact is that masks aren't much use unless they are proper gas masks. 'But surgeons wear masks!' said someone. Indeed they do. But they wear masks to stop the bugs they breathe out contaminating the wound not to stop themselves being contaminated by the air they breathe in.

The Government has made the disease a notifiable disease in order to please travel companies. This is so stupid it is off the stupid-scale. If the disease affects one in four individuals (as has been wildly forecast) then doctors will have to fill in 15 million forms and 15 million forms will have to be filed, processed and shared with various departments. There will be little time for anything else.

Members of the media are having a wonderful time. 'People will die!' screamed the *Daily Mail*. Well, that is probably true. But the whole thing needs to be put into perspective.

Mind you, tabloid newspapers are blamed for scaremongering but these days it's also governments which specialise in scaremongering – as they attempt to terrify us into silent obedience.

It seems to me that the excitement is the AIDS scare all over again. Remember when the BMA warned us that everyone would be affected by the year 2000? TV and newspapers were united in ignoring the facts and promoting the fear. I got into terrible trouble for arguing (accurately) that the fear was exaggerated and that the evidence had been distorted by lobbyists. The nonsense terrified people so much that some committed suicide. Fear is used to oppress and distract. Watch out for compulsory inoculation.

The stock market is behaving as though the disease is going to kill everyone and destroy all commerce. Well, if it does then there won't be any point in holding any shares. But if it doesn't kill us all (or most of us) then the shares will go back up.

March 7th 2020

We clearly haven't been told the truth about the disease.

No Government could possibly be as inept as this one has been in 'managing' this alleged sudden outbreak – unless there was something else going on.

If the Government really wanted to protect us they would have closed airports and banned flights and international travel.

But they didn't.

And why should we trust what we are told?

We all know that Governments lie to the citizens all the time.

Governments lied incessantly about the wars in Iraq, Afghanistan and elsewhere. We were told we were fighting for freedom but everyone with functioning cerebral tissue knows we were fighting for oil.

So, why should we believe what we are told now?

I now suspect that the disease has been outside China for some time – almost certainly for at least a month and probably longer.

And, although I have struggled to suppress my suspicions, I now firmly believe there is a hidden agenda here.

What is it?

Well, actually, there are two.

The first possibility is that governments around the world are going to 'discover' a wonderful inoculation. And it will be compulsory – setting a precedent. Can it really be a coincidence that for months now the authorities (aided by the media) have been demonising anyone who questions the effectiveness and safety of inoculation? All discussion is now banned and in some countries doctors can lose their licences if they dare to question inoculation. (I have, for some years, been banned from all UK media because I have shared the truth about inoculation in my books and articles.)

The second possibility is that the changes introduced as a result of the 'crisis' are designed to get rid of a huge demographic problem: the number of old people in the world. Rising populations and falling birth rates mean that there are huge problems ahead. Who will pay for pensions and health care for the huge numbers of elderly folk around?

Well, one convenient thing about this disease appears to be that it seems to target the elderly. That's unusual. Very few, if any, diseases attack only the elderly. Diseases of this kind usually attack the weak, the frail and the very young. But this one, so we are told, targets the elderly – not just the weakest but all people over 70. And that is very strange.

Is it possible that the infection has been designed to kill off older folk? It would not be difficult to do.

But no one seems to find this strange or worrying.

Indeed, over the last few days, there have been numerous instances of people cheering at the thought of a disease which will kill the old. 'It will clear hospital beds,' said one. 'It only kills oldies,' said another, dismissing the infection as irrelevant. Social media users have been cheering the fact that millions of old people may die.

If someone had said 'It only kills gays' or 'It only affects Arabs' or 'It only targets Jews' – the police would have been on their doorstep in minutes. They would, rightly, have been arrested, charged and thrown into prison.

But you can say what you like about the elderly and no one cares.

Is this the beginning of a great 'cleansing' of modern societies? Get rid of the old folk and preserve the planet for the bright, young things?

I'm afraid my twin fears cannot be dismissed as paranoid delusions.

March 14th 2020

Governments around the world are clearly suffering from mass hysteria. It used to be a problem found mainly among groups of teenage girls. It is now a problem affecting national governments and international organisations.

This isn't anything new, of course.

It has often been governments which have created unnecessary scares – and there has often been a hidden agenda.

And as a medical writer I have frequently found myself trying to defuse the fear created by stupid politicians and civil servants.

I was the only doctor in Britain to oppose the BMA's view that 'AIDS will affect us all'. (I was vilified for disagreeing with the establishment. At its peak, more people were employed as AIDS advisors than had the disease.)

I disagreed with the Government view that Mad Cow Disease would kill half a million or more. (I got into trouble for that though the death toll came to less than 200).

I opposed the Government when it threatened us with death by avian flu. (More trouble for me for daring to question the authorities.) The World Health Organisation claimed that the H5N1 avian flu could kill between five million and 150 million people around the world. In the end the final death total was less than 500.

I opposed the Government when it was claimed that swine flu would kill 65,000 in 2009. (That made me even more unpopular though I was right again. Less than 500 people died, and the Government wasted £500 million of our money on medicines which had to be thrown away. It turned out that the so-called swine flu was no more lethal than ordinary flu.

And on and on it goes. Over the last few decades there have been scares almost every year. And almost every year the establishment has been wrong. They keep picking the wrong things to worry about. And they miss the really big threats.

It annoys me intensely that the world's governments seem determined to create a crisis out of a very small health problem. (What will they do if the plague comes back?) Horrifyingly, in the UK, cancer and heart operations have been cancelled – presumably so that the NHS can prepare itself for the expected onslaught. That is beyond cruel. It is unnecessary and in my view close to criminal in deed if not intent. I am appalled that a number of GPs' surgeries are closing and GPs are telling patients to stay away. Is that not unprofessional and unethical behaviour? (As an aside, I wonder how many doctors will be sued for making diagnostic errors when trying to make diagnoses over the telephone instead of face to face.)

The fact is that the small number of people who have so far died around the world would have almost certainly died of the ordinary flu. In the UK it is not unknown for 50,000 people to die of flu in the winter months. No one takes much notice because most of the people who die are elderly or frail. No one in government cares very much. How many people have so far died of the disease in the UK? How many have died in the world – including China?

It is already apparent that the economic and social consequences of the reaction to the 'crisis' are extreme. Sports events are being cancelled for months ahead. Why? If crowds at sporting events need to be kept away why not play the events just for television? If teams and organisers cared about their sport they would happily do that in order to keep their fans entertained. It would not be difficult to protect players and officials by testing them before and during competitions. But it seems that sport these days is simply about money.

Hundreds of thousands of people are going to be made redundant as a result of companies going bust because of this fake scare. And millions have already seen their pensions and savings decimated. Having the lowest interest rates ever has pushed people to invest in the stock market in order to have any income at all. (Interest rates far below inflation mean that money just disappears if not invested more aggressively than being left in a bank account.) Now those investors are being punished.

Cancelling all public events and elections is utterly absurd. There is no logical explanation for it.

I am convinced that as far as infections are concerned the biggest health problem in Britain is the use of recycling bins. If the Government really believes we have a health problem caused by an infection then we should all be told to put all our rubbish into black bags. Those daft plastic boxes used for recycling are spreading a whole smorgasbord of infections as it is.

Telling people to self-isolate if they have any cold symptoms will cause endless bankruptcies and do nothing to protect the rest of us. And since the disease can last 28 days, self-isolating for 7 days is pointless. The idea that people who self-isolate can keep away from family members in the same home is utterly ludicrous – unless you live in a 58-room mansion.

One thing that is interesting is that the EU members have behaved like a lot of individual countries – looking after themselves. As always, the pen pushers at the EU have been utterly useless in providing leadership. Now they want the rest of the world (including the UK and the US) to find £700 billion to bail out Italy. Neither the EU nor the IMF has enough cash.

The bottom line is that the stress caused by governments' absurd over-reactions will kill far more people. Premature deaths go up with unemployment levels.

In the long term, the best way to create a healthier world is to ban aeroplanes. They carry infections of all kinds around the world. And the people travelling inside planes are all at risk – the air is recycled with the result that if there is one infected person on a plane then all the passengers will have that infection within minutes. Air conditioning systems are equally deadly (and mostly unnecessary).

There is one good thing likely to come out of this: people may learn to cover their mouths when coughing or sneezing in public.

So, what is the hidden agenda? I no longer think it's just about killing off old people. And I don't think the mass enforced inoculation is the sole reason for the scare either.

The scare has to be about money and power.

Get ready for lots of tough new laws. There will probably be travel restrictions. (Never forget the biggest problem facing the world at the moment is the shortage of oil.)

And there will be lots of new taxes. The money will be needed to pay for the chaos caused by the 'crisis' – but the taxes won't be repealed afterwards.

One thing is certain: when this hysterical fiasco is over, you and I will be poorer and have less freedom.

And the Bilderbergers (and their pals) will be richer and have more power.

March 15th 2020

So, now we know what it's all about: it's an excuse for the Government to declare war on the elderly. And the first move in that war is to imprison and isolate everyone over 70.

Whether we like it or not we oldies are going to be locked in for our own good. (It's always for our own good, isn't it?) We are going to be locked in for 'just' four months. But perhaps longer. Maybe permanently.

But it's not really for our sake, is it? They don't give a stuff if we live or die.

They would never dare tell any other group of people that they had to stay in their homes. There would be huge rows and much talk about human rights. But no one gives a damn about the elderly. We're regarded as a useless burden. We've served our purpose, worked and paid taxes, and now we can fade away. We voted to leave the EU and so we must be punished. Dump the old folks on the hillsides and let them quietly die and rot.

In reality, this blatant act of age discrimination has absolutely nothing whatsoever to do with the disease. There are 50-year-olds with respiratory disease who would die if they got within a hundred yards of any flu infection and there are 90-year-olds who run marathons faster than anyone in the Cabinet could open a bottle of gin. They're not locking us in to protect us. They don't give a toss if we live or die. They are locking us in to deny us access to the NHS we paid for. They're locking up the elderly because they can and because we're considered a liability and a bloody nuisance. We get locked in our own homes. No visitors. No contact with the outside world. Ignored and forgotten.

They say we will get our food supplies left on our doorsteps lest we get to see a person and say 'hello'. That's nice of them. Who, pray is going to do all the delivering? Our local supermarkets are already unable to cope with the demand for home deliveries. Volunteers? Don't make me laugh. Most of the volunteering in Britain is done by old folk and they're all going to be locked in.

What are we supposed to do if a delivery does come? Pop out and grab our allocated groceries off the step before they are stolen or soaked in the rain? There will probably be no plastic bags; just a loose pile of groceries sitting there, amidst the dead leaves and the dog-shit, for us to pick up and drag into our homes. Solitary joys will be provided by daytime television. If it's anywhere near as bad as it was when I was a regular 'performer' the days will drag for those who tune in. We won't be allowed to go out to the post box. Those without phones won't be allowed out to use the phone box. We won't be allowed to put out our rubbish because that would mean leaving the house and venturing out into the world. If there are several people living in a house, and one of them is over 70, then they will all be locked in otherwise the rule doesn't make any sense. How many families will survive being locked up for months and months?

They've already told us oldies that we will be denied NHS care. And there won't be any private care because the NHS has bought up all the private beds. We don't qualify for being tested to see if we are infected because we're too old to matter. (The testing is meaningless, by the way. Just because you test 'negative' on Tuesday doesn't mean that you won't test 'positive' on Wednesday.) Some GPs, who will be too busy filling in notifiable disease forms to waste their valuable time on patients, say they won't visit old people. If we fall ill and collapse then we'll be left to die and slowly rot. I wonder if undertakers will be allowed in to collect us. I'm so glad I paid my taxes for more than half a century. The millennials, who have paid little, are the lucky but undeserving recipients of my largesse.

If we dare to step outside our homes we will doubtless be arrested. The world is full of snitches these days. The people who have cameras on their car dashboards will be eager to tell the authorities that the old woman at No 14 has just slipped out in her slippers and hobbled home with fresh bread, a bottle of stout and a jumbo sized packet of aspirin tablets. The poor old sod at no 27 who takes his dog for a brief walk at 1.00 a.m. will be dobbed in too. I wonder if they'll arrest poor Fido too.

The police don't have time to arrest burglars or muggers but I bet they'll find the time to arrest the rebellious old folk who venture out of doors – even if they are taking the dog for a walk or buying in a little food.

As it happens, I don't much mind staying in. We have plenty of books and DVDs. Antoinette and I can both keep busy and amuse ourselves. But I want to stay in because I want to stay in and not because some patronising, bullying, heavy-booted fascist bastards in London tell me I have to stay in.

And I have many reasons why I will need to go out.

The shops and cafes will be closed but I need to see the dentist. I need to visit the optician. I need to visit the bank occasionally to pay in cheques and pay bills. I will, presumably, be denied access to these essential services. Murderers get to see a dentist and an optician. But not the over 70s. I shall want to buy a birthday card for my wife. And, if there are any shops still open, a present too.

Far more importantly, Antoinette (who has breast cancer) needs a mammogram soon (if the NHS has abandoned its collective impersonation of a bunch of headless chickens and is still doing mammograms). She needs to have her B12 injections. She needs to visit the physiotherapist. She has to pick up supplies of her tamoxifen. If Boris and Co think I'm letting her go to the hospital by herself they're pottier than I think they are.

And if we don't drive the car then the battery will be dead and the engine will seize up.

Locking us all in our homes for the solitary sin of being old is something new.

However, in the words of the great and immortal Patrick McGoohan, I am not a prisoner or a number.

I will take Antoinette to her hospital appointments if hospitals are open. I will go to the dentist if dentists are open. I will do what needs to be done. I will decide for myself how I will live my life.

What are they going to do if we all ignored the law?

There's a problem the bastards haven't thought of.

What will they do with their prisoners? Shackle them? Put them in prison? Fit them with those ankle bracelets used for criminals and terrorists?

We can't go to court if we're arrested and charged because we aren't allowed to leave our homes.

March 16th 2020

The World Health Organisation estimates that the number of people dying from 'seasonal influenza' each year is between 290,000 and 650,000.

It's worth repeating: in a bad year, well over half a million people die from the flu. In one bad winter month, the death toll from flu could approach 100,000.

That's not the number who get it. That's the number who die from it.

And the infection which is the cause of our global 'crisis'?

Well, today (the 16th March) the official figure is that just over 6,500 people have died of it since the first diagnosis was made. It's difficult to know when that was. Some authorities claim that it was last November. Others say it was January. But if we are cautious and say that the disease didn't start killing people until a month ago then the disease has, in that time, killed 6,500 people. That's the global figure – which includes China. In a bad year the flu would (at this time of the year) have killed more than ten times as many people. I'm just providing the facts.

Some authorities claim that the 'ordinary' flu is easier to catch.

And the USA's Centers for Disease Control and Prevention estimates that up to 45 million people a year catch the flu. The new disease will have to accelerate at quite a pace to get anywhere near that figure.

A reader of my website telephoned the Department of Health in London and asked if they could tell him, 'how many people are dying of flu at this time'. They couldn't. And they would only reply if the query were offered as an official freedom of information request. That is astonishing. It seems that the Government doesn't have figures for the number of people with the flu but it can provide almost hourly figures for the number with a much less common infection. Maybe the figures for the number dying of flu are mixed in with the number dying of the new disease. After all, very few people are being tested, the symptoms of the two diseases are pretty well identical and a doctor writing a death certificate is quite likely to put down the new disease rather than 'influenza' because the new disorder is notifiable and he/she has been influenced by the media hysteria.

As I pointed out on March 2nd, the mortality figures for the new disease are also probably distorted because statisticians and journalists divide the number of deaths into the number of recorded cases to find the death rate. But these figures are worthless because the number of people who actually have the infection (and merely deal with their symptoms at home) is inevitably far, far higher than the number who have reported to their doctor and far higher than the number who have tested positive. It is worth pointing out that the NHS is now only testing people who are actually in hospital (and, by definition) very ill, and has apparently banned private testing. (I only know this because top professional football clubs were complaining that they weren't allowed to get their players tested privately.) All this enables the authorities to do pretty much what they like with the figures.

Many, many years ago I pointed out that the mortality figures for AIDS were being distorted because deaths from tuberculosis and a whole host of other diseases were being included in the official

AIDS figures. The authorities needed the figures to be higher to justify the scaremongering and the vast amounts of money that had been spent on the disease. It seems to me that the same thing is happening now. Who will ever know the difference?

Italy is often quoted as the worst country in Europe for getting and dying of the new disease. But far fewer people have died in Italy of it than would have died of the flu in a fairly normal year. And that doesn't allow for the fact that many of the alleged deaths were probably flu deaths. Incidentally, it has been said that the 'crisis' in Italy is now so bad that doctors are saying they can no longer treat the over 80s – whatever is wrong with them. Golly, isn't that a surprise. This is exactly what has been said in Britain – though the cut off age is lower.

According to leaked NHS figures, the new disease will put eight million Britons into hospital and 80% of the nation will become infected. Who the hell made up these figures? You might as well claim that it will kill 90% of all citizens whose names begin with A. It's meaningless drivel. The newspapers are reporting this nonsense as though it were real.

Some of the rules being introduced are stark raving bonkers. So, footballers have been told not to shake hands before a game. But they then run around hugging and holding one another.

So far all the people who have died of the new disease in the UK had underlying health issues. The youngest to date was 59 – rather proving my argument that it is nonsensical to lock up the over 70s. If the Government wants to lock people into their homes then it should lock in those who have underlying health issues – whatever their age. The fact that the Government has selected the over 70s for locking in rather proves the point that this is all about isolating, dehumanising and marginalising the elderly.

My conclusion is that the 'crisis' is being used to get people used to the idea that the elderly cannot be treated. Governments around the world can no longer afford to pay pensions. It is well known that aging populations are a real threat to the economies of a number of countries. Was the 'crisis' designed to enable governments to get rid of the elderly? Or are governments merely taking opportunistic advantage of the infection to marginalise old folk?

In my sixth diary (*The Game's Afoot*) I pointed out that Governments everywhere have been trying to kill off the elderly for years. Don't believe me? What about the Liverpool Care Pathway which originated in Britain? That was the murderers' charter, which allowed doctors and nurses to withhold food, water and essential treatment from patients who are over 65 and who are, therefore, regarded as an expensive nuisance. The Liverpool Care Pathway was then replaced by something called Sustainable Development Goals (which originated with the United Nations). Sustainable Development Goals allows the NHS to discriminate against anyone over the age of 70 on the grounds that people who die when they are over 70 cannot be said to have died 'prematurely' and so will not count when the nation's healthcare is being assessed. The Government loves this new rule because it gives the State permission to get rid of citizens who are of pensionable age and, therefore, regarded by society's accountants as a 'burden'. It is hardly surprising, I suppose, that this officially sponsored disdain for the elderly has trickled through into our courts. If you mug a 40-year-old you are likely to go to prison for a good length of time. But if you mug and kill an 80-year-old you will be unlucky if you go to prison for more than a few months. The lives of the elderly do not count for much.

There have to be priorities within the health service. There isn't enough money for everything but although there is plenty of cash for cosmetic surgery and gender reassignment programmes, the NHS has little money for treating macular degeneration – which causes blindness in old people. The elderly are discriminated against without anyone seeming to notice or care. Successive British governments seem to have decided that the elderly are surplus to requirements. Pensions are kept pitifully small. (The UK's State pension is the worst in any developed economy.) Energy prices have been allowed to soar so that subsidies can be given to climate change programmes with the result that tens of thousands of older people die of the cold because they can't afford to eat and to keep warm.

I find myself toying with all sorts of strange scenarios. Nothing now seems impossible.

In a couple of months' time, will campaigners use the 'crisis' as an excuse to demand a rerun of the EU referendum – on the grounds that the elderly who voted for Brexit are now safely locked up in their homes and unable to get out to the polling stations?

Impossible?

Wouldn't you have thought it impossible that the Government would order all citizens over the age of 70 to stay in their homes for four months because of a new infection which is killing less people than the flu?

Nothing now seems impossible.

One main aim seems to be to demonise, marginalise and dehumanise the elderly so that governments have an excuse to stop providing health care for the over 70s.

The young who seem to welcome the idea of the elderly being deprived of medical care might like to reflect on two thoughts. First, they may one day be old themselves. Second, the age for cutting off medical services will get younger and younger – as the pension age gets older and older. Today's 20-year-olds may well find that they are ineligible for medical care when they hit 50.

March 19th 2020

Foolishly, on the 18th March I recorded a YouTube video to provide some facts about the 'crisis'. It was a huge mistake. I did not monetise my YouTube channel because the video was made purely to try to offer another view of the alleged 'crisis'. I did not promote the video or use it to advertise or promote anything other than my website – which is free and carries no advertisements.

After just one day, the video had received over 100,000 views. But when the Government changed a few things (they reduced the quarantine for the elderly to three months, they did what I had suggested and told those with chronic illnesses to stay indoors and they told those who had cold symptoms to stay indoors for 14 days instead of 7 days) I took down the original video and recorded a new one with the correct details. I believe that accuracy is always important when offering criticism or a review.

But that was another huge mistake.

Unknown to me, the original video had been taken by people who had put my video (in its entirety) up on their own websites. I had recorded the video as a public service, not wanting to make any money out of it, but these people were clearly cashing in and a number of them had used my video to attract advertising. Both Antoinette and I were horrified. I have for decades refused to accept adverts or sponsorship of any kind so I was appalled to see that my work was now festooned with all sorts of adverts.

Antoinette and I spent almost an entire day trying to persuade these people to take down my video. I very politely pointed out that the video they were showing was now out-of-date and an embarrassment to me and to them. I even told them that if they took down the out-of-date video then they could put up the new video which I had recorded.

Worse still, when checking these sites we found that I had been the object of a massive amount of personal abuse.

My sole aim had been to provide a voice of cautious reason in an increasingly hysterical world. But I was accused of trying to grab my five minutes of fame (I was moderately famous a few decades ago and that was more than enough) and I was accused of being a 'quack' (a clear libel since I am not). I was abused and criticised for just about everything imaginable.

My wife Antoinette, who was helping (without success) to try to control the thefts, was horrified by what she read. We both immediately decided that we would never again read any comments put on the bottom of a video.

I am sad that good intentions brought such a harvest of abuse. It seems that offering an alternative view is no longer acceptable and attracts a strange mixture of oppressive intolerance and belligerent playground rudeness.

March 21st 2020

It occurs to me that the hoarding which is now commonplace in Britain is being made far, far worse by the media coverage. It is pretty well established that papers and television don't show pictures of streakers because it encourages more to follow suit. So why hasn't the Government issued a D notice telling the media not to print pictures of people with overloaded trolleys or of empty supermarket shelves? If you constantly show pictures of empty shelves then people will panic – and feel they have to stock up with everything they can find.

A month ago, it was predicted that 500,000 or even 600,000 people might die during this 'crisis' in Britain. Then the figure quietly fell to 400,000 and to 260,000. However, according to a story buried inside the *Daily Telegraph*, the experts now appear to be predicting a death toll in Britain of 20,000. This is considerably less than the death rate which might be expected from a nasty strain of the flu. Why wasn't this news on the front page? Maybe health secretary Matt Hancock would like to calm the fear he created by predicting a possible death total of 500,000.

Some 'experts' appear to have reported that 3.4% of patients will die. But the World Health Organization has pointed out that the 3.4% death rate is a result of measuring the number of deaths against the number of reported cases and does not account for the possibility that there may be lots more people infected with the bug– but undiagnosed. I seem to have been making that point for half a lifetime (and being abused for it). It now seems that the death rate is probably rather less than 1%. This is not all that far off the death rate we get every year with the flu. The death rate in China (where the infection started) has already started to fall noticeably.

If the death rate in the UK is lower than originally forecast, the Prime Minister will doubtless claim it is because of the actions he has taken. 'But he would say that, wouldn't he?'

A couple of aggrieved but inevitably anonymous Wikipedians have asked Wikipedia to remove my Wikipedia entry. It seems that my views on the 'crisis' are considered too controversial and too much out of step with the authorities for me to be allowed a Wikipedia page – though I believe Adolf Hitler has one. I am told that the Wikipedia world is desperately upset by my views. Their complaints about me are absurdly libellous and they have changed the site to make me seem deranged. They have, for example, listed a number of complaints made against me by a private body called the Advertising Standards Authority. The ASA accepted a complaint from the meat industry which was triggered by an advert for my book, *Food for Thought* – which rightly lists meat as a cause of cancer. I sent the ASA a list of 26 scientific papers which proved that I was right but they refused to look at them. That all happened about 25 years ago so is hardly front page news. Since then every government in the world, and the WHO, have all agreed that everything I said was right. But the Wikipedians merely note that the ASA disagreed.

Self-styled experts are popping up all over the place. It has again been pointed out that the disease might mutate again and become more deadly and/or more infectious. That is true. It might happen tomorrow, but we might have to wait years before that happens. How long do we all stay indoors and wait for a possible mutation? Weeks? Months? Years? And just how much damage to our society and economy will have been done by then?

When the Government asked retired doctors to help out, I wrote to the General Medical Council asking what I had to do to reinstate my licence to practise. They wrote back to say that since my email address had changed they wouldn't do anything until I had my passport scanned and sent to them by email. Good to see that the GMC is maintaining its reputation for bureaucracy. We don't have a working scanner (the last three all died) and anyway there is not a chance in hell of my sending a copy of my passport to anyone by email. Still, the world will probably be a safer place if I stay at home. And I have no idea where my stethoscope is. And I am apparently too old to be considered to be useful anyway. So that idea was stillborn.

March 22nd 2020

In the US, the Centers for Disease Control and Prevention reports that so far this flu season at least 36 million Americans have caught the flu, 370,000 have been hospitalized and 22,000 have died. Those are the figures for America alone. I mention this simply to try to put things in perspective. As I write, the number of cases of the new disease worldwide is just in excess of 300,000 and the number of global deaths is just over 13,000. The new disease is nasty and dangerous. But so is the flu and I don't remember any governments ever shutting down a country because of the flu.

Now that Antoinette and I have been instructed to stay indoors, I have ordered a yellow quarantine flag (ex Royal Navy) to fly on our flagpole.

There seems to be a widespread misunderstanding of the word 'pandemic' among my most frothy mouthed critics. I assume they are too busy sneering to find themselves a dictionary. A pandemic is a widespread disease. A global pandemic is simply a disease which is widespread over the whole world. The word doesn't mean that the disease is particularly lethal. It is not uncommon for there to be flu pandemics. For the record, 'endemic' means that a disease is commonly found in a particular area or among a certain group of people. And an 'epidemic' is the widespread occurrence of an infectious disease in a community.

In the last couple of days I have received four requests to appear on the radio. Two invitations came from the USA, one from an Arab country and one from Mexico. None was from British stations. The only time I hear from the BBC is when they write 'requesting' that I pay their absurdly out-of-date licence fee. They do this once a month. The BBC's demand for their licence fee was sneakily designed to look like one of those little cards which the Royal Mail leaves when they have a parcel for you but you weren't in.

I still suspect that, as with climate change, the 'cure' to this 'crisis' will do more lasting harm than the disease. The chaos is getting worse. When the over 70s were told to stay indoors they were assured that food would be delivered and placed on their doorsteps. Unfortunately, everyone is now ordering their food online, and the elderly have been told that they can do their shopping in the supermarket at a time when it will be crammed to the doors with loads of other elderly folk doing their shopping. Some of those shoppers will have the disease but social distancing will be impossible. Incidentally, the habit of NHS staff doing their shopping in their uniforms suggests a complete failure to understand how bugs spread. If supermarkets want to help their customers they should ban NHS staff from entering their stores while wearing clothes they wore while working with patients.

Scaremongers are now telling us that young, healthy adults have died of the disease. It is worth remembering that young, healthy adults can and do die from the flu.

What the devil will a future government do if there is an outbreak of a real killer infection such as the plague or Ebola fever? And will the people take any notice of the warnings? How many times can a government cry wolf and expect the citizens to listen?

There are a good many false stories around. There is, for example, an article going the rounds which claims that the disease causing the 'crisis' is known to 'eat lungs'. I don't think that sort of emotive imagery does a great deal of good. The disease can certainly damage the lungs. But this disease doesn't eat lungs – that's the munchy munchy lurgy which starred in a movie made by Hammer Films in the 1960s.

A friend of Antoinette's who lives in Germany and has seen the news kindly asked if we needed supplies sending over. I sent a message back that we have baked beans and loo rolls but could do with another bottle of 10-year-old Laphroaig and perhaps one of 12-year-old Bunnahabhain.

March 24th 2020

I've been studying inoculation programmes for over 50 years and I would be surprised if I don't know more about them than my many pro-inoculation critics, who seem to believe that anything in a syringe which is recommended by the Government must be good for you. Sadly, however, ignorance doesn't seem to stop the pro-inoculation enthusiasts from airing their opinions, though they appear more adept at offering abuse than they are at offering scientific evidence for their views. The abuse I am receiving continues. (AIDS, inoculations and the new disease attract more fury from the ignorant and the opinionated than any other health subjects.) I wish I had never written a word about this damned 'crisis'.

Prices of things online seem to have soared. Today, I bought hazelnuts for the squirrels (who are always hungry at this time of year) and paid twice the price I paid a couple of weeks ago. Heaven knows what the price will be in another fortnight. Even basic home medicines seem to be rising in price and that certainly isn't fair.

Worse still, I was horrified almost beyond words to read that surgery for cancer patients has been delayed for two weeks because of the 'crisis'. I could weep. The physical and mental stress on patients with cancer who are waiting for surgery is unimaginable. Who the hell made this decision? Cancer is not a fringe disease; it causes more than a quarter of all deaths in the UK and I don't mind betting that in the end this decision will cause considerably more deaths than the 'crisis' disease. I know from our experience just how stressful it can be to have to wait for tests, results and treatment. I bet patients with suspected cancer are also having to wait longer for scans and for their scans to be read.

It is no exaggeration to say that the medical profession appears to have gone mad.

Doctors have been given the right to discharge elderly patients early to free up beds. Since the over 70s have to stay at home and are not allowed visitors to care for them just who, pray, will look after these lonely, old people? Many will not be able to go to the shops for food, many won't have access to the internet and so won't be able to shop online. It is not widely realised but, according to the Office for National Statistics more than five million people have never gone online. Within a month or so some of these will starve to death.

It is now being said that we could all be quarantined and isolated for 18 months or until herd immunity reaches 60%-70%. If everyone has to stay indoors for 18 months there will be more murders and divorces than at any previous time in history. And we will no longer have a working economy.

Here's a thought: instead of forcing those without the disease to lock themselves in, wouldn't it make more sense to lock all those who are ill (and those with whom they have been in contact and who may be symptomless but who test positive) into isolation hospitals or hotels converted into isolation hospitals. This would cause less disruption. Who could possibly object to that? Oh, and we should close our borders completely. (This is something I recommended weeks ago – at the time when Putin closed Russia's borders. If we had closed our borders, or isolated people coming into the country, we would probably not need a general lockdown.)

Figures from around the world continue to bemuse me. It is said that 9,000 people in Iran are infected and that 300 have died. That would give a death rate of over 3%. But it also said that there may actually be 100,000 infected. That would give a death rate of around 0.3%. I don't think any more figures should be released until there is some certainty about them.

When the dust settles, France is going to go bankrupt. Macron has promised that no company, of any size, will be allowed to go bankrupt. All those directors whose companies were previously close to bankruptcy will be beaming.

Are we locked in? Locked up? Or in lock down? Whatever it is, I am so pleased that we are all allowed an exercise period though there will be guards to keep an eye on us. Just like proper prison. I am puzzled though. The police and guards are to be allowed to fine those who break the law by forming groups outside. This is doubtless sensible but how will the police hand a summons or fine to the individuals concerned without touching them or approaching them? And if they wear protective clothing they will have to change every time they fine someone.

Last night, Antoinette made up a large boxful of comestibles to take to an old lady we know who lives alone. (Antoinette also popped one of our valuable loo rolls into the box – in my view an unprecedented act of generosity.) Nervously, I drove several miles through deserted streets. It was a cross between Christmas Day and a scene in one of those films in which a killer plague destroys the world. When we arrived we put the box into the porch, rang the bell and ran away in case anyone had seen us. It is, of course, illegal for me to be out of the house except to do essential shopping or take my statutory exercise.

The Germans were apparently told to stock up with food for at least two weeks. The British are told that we must not stock up but that we should go to the shops as infrequently as possible. It is impossible to do both. It would make more sense for everyone to buy infrequently but to buy as much as they can carry. Given the difficulty in obtaining delivery slots, the supermarkets will surely have to start delivering 24 hours a day. (That's another suggestion I offer to our Leaders.) Antoinette and I did not 'panic buy' but I confess I rather wish we had more stuff in our pantry.

Many over 70s are terrified of falling ill and needing a doctor. I know I am. Even falling over and breaking a bone is now a constant terror – because of the problems of obtaining medical care, and the knowledge that as an elderly patient there may be difficulty in obtaining medical care. The NHS needs to reassure the over 70s that they will not be ignored if they need help. But that's not going to happen because they will be ignored.

March 25th 2020

The local hospital rang Antoinette this morning to cancel her next physiotherapy appointment. Apparently, the hospital is closing its doors to sick people. I found this a little odd because it's a small hospital with no A&E and no ITU beds. Still, I have long waited for the day when hospitals decided it was better not to let the corridors and wards get filled up with poorly people. I wonder how many millions of other people in pain are being told that their hospital appointment is cancelled.

I am astonished that the only people being tested are the seriously ill who are in hospital. Epidemiologically, we need to know how many people have had the infection (with or without symptoms) in order to make plans.

We are convinced that Antoinette had the infection. A while ago she was coughed on in a health food store by a Chinese fellow (that's a pertinent fact, not a racist remark) and a few days later she developed symptoms. The cough was so bad she damaged ribs on her healthy side and has a good deal of pain there. The tissues on her left side are burnt up by the radiotherapy and scarred by surgery and the tissues on her right side are damaged by coughing.

I spent ages today trying to get through to the Sainsbury hotline to report myself as being an elderly person – in the hope that we could then book a supermarket delivery. It would have been easier to get through to the tax office. All I got was an occasional message telling me to do what the Government tells me to do and stay indoors. I don't suppose anyone in the Government saw the irony in that. We can't get a food delivery but we have to stay indoors. Having spent most of the day ringing the priority delivery number (to try to order food) I eventually got a recorded message which told me I had to go to gov.uk to register. I went to gov.uk but after ten minutes I gave up – having failed to find anywhere to register. And what, pray, about the five million people (most of them elderly) who do not have access to the internet? I have to say that the Government in Britain has made a complete hash of caring for its citizens. It had plenty of time to organise adequate phone and food delivery services as originally promised but it has failed dismally. It would have been easy to use existing call centres to provide folk with a place to obtain information. And, for heaven's sake, we live at a time when the Government knows everything about us. Why not just tell the supermarkets who the over 70s are? For millions, it'll be fried carpet for dinner until someone in the Government works out that if you lock everyone in you have to make an effort to keep them alive.

Unless, of course, you don't want them to stay alive. But that's the thought that got me into trouble in the first place.

Another thought: we need more self-service check out points in supermarkets to avoid putting supermarket cashiers in the firing line – having to confront hundreds of people face to face. Testing supermarket cashiers should be a priority over testing celebrities and footballers. Surely the self-service check out points that aren't being used in shops which are closed could be moved into supermarkets.

The big danger in this 'crisis' is pneumonia. That's what kills. And it is, of course, the same reason that flu kills. Oh, and by the way the flu constantly mutates in the same way that the new disease is probably going to mutate. It's the ever changing nature of the flu which explains why the flu jab often doesn't work at all.

I see that a study at Oxford University has concluded that the new infection could have already infected half the British population and been spreading in the UK since January. Professor Sunetra Gupta, Professor of Theoretical Epidemiology said we need more testing to find out where we are in the epidemic. But tragically and inexplicably the Government is only testing people who are seriously ill in hospital. The danger is that those numbers will distort the picture massively. Dr Gupta is reported to have told the *Financial Times* that she was surprised that there had been such unqualified acceptance of the views from Imperial College in London – the views upon which Government policy has been based. If Dr Gupta is right then my original predictions were also exactly right.

I still believe many governments have panicked. I believe the 'cure' will be worse than the 'disease'. I could be wrong, of course. But my worry is that, if I am right, when will the Government have the courage to cancel its lock-in policies? Or will they continue and then, in a few months' time, say: 'There you are, we saved you all. By the way, income tax is going to be doubled next April.'

I feel so sorry for children who are not only losing invaluable school days but who will 'lose' a birthday in the next few weeks or months. No presents or cards or balloons or cakes or party.

As I predicted the other day, our local council is threatening to suspend bin collections. Never miss an opportunity to save money at the expense of the citizens. They are, however, continuing with the recycling collections – thereby massively increasing the risks of cross infection but reducing their penalty payments to the European Union. That's the second most stupid thing they've done. The most stupid thing they have done is to close all the parks to stop people taking exercise. I rather thought we were all allowed a brief exercise period every day. The council appears to have decided otherwise. Watch out for a rise in obesity, heart attacks and diabetes.

Antoinette has been in tears for days, already tired and weak from her breast cancer and the treatments for it and now depressed by the deluge of abuse, lies, distortions and malicious libels which have been coming my way. I've been writing about medical matters for a long, long time and, to be honest, I'm weary of illogical, unfair, venomous criticism from people who have well-formed opinions and a lot of prejudice but very little knowledge. We are going to turn off our phones, abandon the internet and batten down the hatches against a bewildering and inexplicably unkind world where absurdities now seem commonplace and where, among politicians, common sense is as rare as honesty. I hope someone remembers to tell us when it's safe to come out again.

March 26th 2020

I wasn't going to say this but bugger it, I have been savaged for a month because of my comments on this website and then on my YouTube video so I think I have the right to say it.

'I was right!'

It has just been revealed that on March 19th (four days before the lockdown started!) the public health bodies in the UK and the Advisory Committee on Dangerous Pathogens decided that the new disease should no longer be classified as a 'high consequence infectious disease'.

The Government buried this information on their website. Go onto gov.uk and look for 'High consequence infectious diseases (HCID)' for the evidence. The decision to downgrade it was made on 19th March but not published until 21st March.

The disease has been rightly downgraded to an infectious disease – like the flu.

Maybe we can now all have our lives back and try to rescue what is left of Britain.

And then maybe the Government would like to explain how they got it so wrong, what the hidden agenda was and why they put the country into lockdown days after they knew that the infection was not the big killer they had been claiming it to be.

Regular readers will know that right from the start I have reported on www.vernoncoleman.com that I did not believe that the new infection seemed to me to be more threatening than a nasty type of flu.

It was just a point of view, based on many decades of investigating and writing about medical matters. And I gave my reasoning, based on solid, factual evidence available to everyone.

I also expressed some views on why I thought that the problem was being exaggerated.

The Government has also stated that 'Cases of (the infection) are no longer managed by HICD treatment centres only'.

(A high consequence infectious disease is defined as an acute infectious disease which typically has a high case-fatality rate and which requires an enhanced individual, population and system response to ensure it is managed effectively, efficiently and safely. There are a few other requirements but those will do for here. The new infection was one of those. Now it is not.)

Astonishingly, the Government rather buried this information on their website. You have to hunt around, but it's there. And although the decision to downgrade was made on 19th March, it doesn't seem to have been published until 21st March.

Why the delay, I wonder? Were there discussions with the committees about their decisions?

A few days later the country was put into lockdown. The key word there is 'after'.

Naively, this morning I rather expected that the world would be cheering. I thought the lockdown would be lifted, share prices would soar and people would start returning to their lives.

But no one else seems to have reported this news.

And then I found out what was going on.

Today, the Government published an 'Emergency Bill.

The new Bill gives the Government tremendous powers including 'easing legislative and regulatory requirements.

The Bill is 358 pages long and, for a start, lasts two years. They didn't write a 358-page Bill in a week, did they? How long have they been working on this? I would guess that they have been preparing this Bill for at least six months – probably longer.

The police and immigration officers will have new powers.

There is a 'temporary modification of mental health and mental capacity legislation'.

That's a corker.

Secondary certificates are no longer required for cremations.

Hospitals get all sorts of powers.

Public meetings and demonstrations are banned, of course. (No wonder they were so quick to cancel the May elections. They knew this was coming. They could have held purely postal vote elections but they chose not to. Will there be any elections next year?)

There are powers relating to 'restrictions on use and disclosure of information'.

And, lo and behold, there is a note about 'arrangements for the inoculation or immunisation of persons against any disease'.

That probably won't come as much of a surprise to readers of my website. (That prediction was the main source of the criticism poured down upon my ancient head.)

Oh, and Parliament is now closed a week early.

And so Boris Johnson is in charge of the country. Stalin would be green with envy.

I suspect we might have to kiss goodbye to Brexit. It will be claimed that we all have to work together with other countries and that there isn't time to fix a Brexit deal. The ecstatic banks will all be bailed out (again). The EU's long-term plan to get rid of small businesses will be successful at last. When will cash be banned so that they can keep an eye on all our spending and whereabouts? Travel will be controlled and limited.

March 31st 2020

I am (to say the least) surprised that the mainstream media has ignored the biggest story of my lifetime: the decision to downgrade the 'crisis' and the decision, a couple of days later, to introduce the most oppressive Bill in Parliament's history. It appeared on my website but nowhere else that I could see. I certainly couldn't find any mention of this astonishing event on the BBC website and although a dear friend of mine sent details of the story to just about all the national newspapers, I don't think any of them used it. They certainly didn't give it the front page coverage it merited.

Are we to assume that we will be put into lockdown whenever a new flu appears?

Is it any coincidence that since I published the truth about what is going on, I have been monstered, lied about, libelled and traduced all over the internet? My website, which has been readily available for a quarter of a century, is now almost impossible to find. The message seems clear: the truth must be suppressed at all cost.

I have lost count of the number of times attempts have been made to destroy what is left of my reputation. When I argued that AIDS wasn't going to kill us all (as we had been told by the medical establishment) I was attacked by those who had a vested interest in promoting the scare. When I persuaded the Government to put stricter controls on the prescribing of benzodiazepines, I was wildly vilified by doctors working for the drug companies. And so on and so on.

I was not going to write any more about the 'crisis' (hoping that the big media players would have the courage to share the truth with their readers) but the failure of TV, radio, newspapers and big websites to run the story led Antoinette to persuade me to carry on. There has also been disturbingly little coverage of the Oxford University study which concluded that the disease could have already infected half the British population. I strongly suspect that this study is correct. If it is then Government policy is surely wrong. But the Government won't know whether or not it is right because for reasons which I cannot understand, the testing programme is still restricted and minute. We should be testing, testing, testing. Every household in the country should have, by now, been sent a testing kit.

The Government's policy is causing chaos and confusion.

On the one hand we are told that we must go out of the house as little as possible. But on the other hand it is nigh on impossible to obtain supermarket delivery slots. And even when slots are available, customers are only allowed a limited number of items. The exercise regulations are causing confusion too. Originally, the Government said that we could go out and exercise once a day. But the police (who were given real fascist powers in the Bill I described, and who are already enjoying using them) appear to have decided that it is illegal for anyone to go out in their car to find a nice place for a walk. One reason for this restriction was said to be that if people were allowed to wander about, some of them might fall off cliffs and require emergency medical care – putting emergency service staff at risk. I wonder how many people fall off cliffs each year. A dozen, perhaps? How many thousands will have heart attacks through not taking any exercise?

Embarrassed Government ministers immediately agreed with the constabulary and announced that we should not find nice places to go for a walk but should walk in our gardens. Those who live in flats are presumably expected to limit themselves to a wander around their window box.

People in the US and Australia are selling packet soup to British buyers and the prices are obscene. It is now possible to pay £20 to £40 for a packet of soup. Some of the sellers are inviting prospective soup drinkers to bid for one packet of soup. 'War-time' profiteering is back.

I am told that elderly patients in hospital are being encouraged to sign DNR (Do Not Resuscitate) forms. I am not surprised.

The Government has repeated its official prediction that the death total in the UK from the 'crisis' could hit 20,000. (The figure has been gradually downgraded from 500,000.) I wonder how many people know that the average total of deaths caused by flu in England alone is 17,000 a year. That's the average in a normal year. When the flu is bad the figure is much, much higher. And I wonder how many people will die because of the restrictions, the delayed operations, the lost jobs, the poor diets, the lack of exercise and the massive amounts of stress. My guess (and at least I am honest enough to admit it is a guess) is that between 100,000 and 250,000 people will die unnecessarily as a direct result of the 'cure' which the Government has introduced. Just think of all those now being denied essential screening, scanning, treatment and surgery while the NHS devotes itself to an infectious disease in the same epidemiological bracket as the flu. (Curiously, it is still a notifiable disease!) Think of all those who will have heart attacks because they are eating badly and not exercising. Millions will suffer mental and physical disease which will take years to unravel. How long could all this go on for? Presumably, until everyone in the country has acquired immunity and that could take a year or more. What sort of county will we be left with?

Meanwhile, the Government continues to bring in more oppressive laws and the ramifications seem endless. The Emergency Bill that was conveniently prepared and passed last Wednesday (with only minimal scrutiny) has turned Britain into a police state. The police and local council officials have even been trying to stop shops selling Easter eggs lest children have a moment or two of joy over the coming Christian holiday. Bizarrely, washing a car became a criminal offence. There are now calls for identity cards to be introduced though I find it difficult to see why ID cards should help prevent the flu. Why don't the authorities go all the way and tattoo numbers on our forearms. All this is very 1984. Power corrupts and absolute power corrupts absolutely.

Another worry I have is that if cars aren't taken out for a drive of twenty minutes or so every week or two then batteries will go flat and the cars won't start. I need the car to be able to take Antoinette to the pharmacy to collect her medicines and to the doctors' surgery to have her B12 injection. And that is a more serious worry. Antoinette is terrified that she won't be allowed to have her two monthly jabs – without which the painful, neurological symptoms of pernicious anaemia will come bouncing back. And there is also a real risk that the breast cancer will be triggered back into action. Moreover, the nation's hospitals appear to have pretty well closed and I am terrified that Antoinette might need help. And what about her mammogram in a month or so? It's a safe bet that will be delayed. Millions of people are in the same unpleasant situation.

We had a Tesco delivery recently. The young man who brought our modest allowance of groceries was clearly terrified and spoke (from a very safe distance) of things getting a lot worse before they improved. He (sensibly) insisted on signing the electronic device which records receipt of our groceries but I still had to handle the plastic trays in which the food was packed. If the supermarkets are taking this seriously then all groceries being delivered should be packed into plastic bags not the usual plastic trays.

It occurred to me today that Guantanamo Bay is now probably the safest place on earth. (That is the one that Obama was going to shut down on his first day in office. Sadly, he found himself too busy bombing foreign countries, collecting peace prizes and planning his route to untold riches to bother with pre-election promises.)

Dustmen (sorry, 'community recycling consultants') are talking of stopping work and the local council is going to tell us about collections the day before – presumably on the grounds that we aren't allowed out of our homes so what does it matter. People in flats and terraced houses will not be able to cope if rubbish collections are stopped. And the health hazard will be enormous – especially as the weather gets warmer. The rats, already huge, will soon be bigger than policemen, though probably not as bossy.

Britain's Prime Minister is threatening to bring in even tougher laws though to be honest apart from setting up firing squads I cannot think what else he might plan. I have seen spokespersons of one sort or another claiming that the lockdown might last six months, twelve months or eighteen months. In some ways, it feels as though Corbyn had won the last election and turned Britain into a communist state. There is a shortage of food and loo rolls and the shops and restaurants are all shut. This could be the Soviet Union or East Germany in the 1970s. I remember visiting East Berlin in the 1970s and being astonished at the empty shelves in the shops. But at least they had shops which were open.

Today a Government minister announced that the worst is yet to come and that if shoppers aren't more cautious then rationing will have to be introduced. I cannot think of anything more guaranteed to encourage panic buying than the threat of rationing. Is there anyone in the Government with any functioning brain tissue?

Antoinette's rib pain that was triggered by her coughing a while ago is still there and, not surprisingly, Antoinette is worried sick that the cancer has spread into her bones – specifically her ribs. The bones are a favourite target for wandering breast cancer cells. The pain was triggered by bad coughing. It got a little better but it hasn't gone away. The coughing is the cause. But will the hospital see us if we need to ring for help for another problem? From everything I have seen on the news it seems that doctors and hospitals are totally obsessed with this superstar disease. Unbelievably, cancer patients are taking second place. Antoinette paints most days; it is her one way to forget and to find some inner peace.

We were battered by strong winds over the last couple of days and rather than call a builder in I did a few odd jobs myself. I secured the entrance to our wigwam greenhouse with a piece of string and half a dozen rusty, old horseshoes. And I temporarily mended a heavy cast iron downpipe with the aid of a plastic strimmer blade and an iron Victorian foot scraper. But what happens if we really do need a builder? Are we allowed to call in someone if a chunk of roof flies off? Is there anyone to call? Or do we just shrug and put up an umbrella?

Although we managed to get our previously customary Tesco delivery in what has now become the great Phone Lottery, we still haven't heard from Sainsbury's about their much publicised delivery arrangements for the over 70s. If we cannot fix Tesco we were hoping to book a Sainsbury delivery. However, I am beginning to think that this was just a publicity stunt. I have been trying to register for their home deliveries for about a week and so far I have got nowhere. I wrote to gov.uk to complain and received, as expected, a standardised reply which was of absolutely no value. The Government knows where we all live, how old we are, what we earn and what we own. They certainly also know our national insurance numbers. All this information is used quickly and easily to chase us down if we owe sixpence in tax, so why can't the same information be used to make sure that old folk get the food deliveries they were promised?

The newspapers are full of the news that 200 people died today. This is enormously sad but the figure is announced as if it were 200,000. Actually, I see that someone has resurrected the threat that at least 500,000 of us are going to die within a few months. I know of absolutely no evidence for this claim. The scaremongers might just as well claim that five million are going to die. Or why not tell us that we are all going to die and be done with it? Why doesn't someone point out that in an average year the flu kills 20,000 people in the winter season. That means that the average death rate from the ordinary old-fashioned flu in an ordinary year is around 200 a day. In a bad year it will be much higher than that. Every time a previously healthy individual dies, that is offered as evidence that the new disease is far more deadly than the flu. But it is also important to remember that the ordinary flu also kills previously healthy individuals.

I see that Tony Blair is giving us the benefit of his wisdom. Very nice of him since he usually provides his thoughts to rich American banks who can afford his massive fees. If he is going to pitch in with his half-penny's worth we might as well go round the prisons and invite other mass murderers to offer us their advice. Maybe the Yorkshire Ripper has a view. What the hell does Blair know about anything other than deceit and betrayal? I understand that he has a need to appear on television regularly but why do TV companies keep giving him airtime?

It was reported that a man had died after touching a currency note that was infected. Congratulations to whoever managed to prove that a patient died from a banknote – even if the note was tested and turned out to be contaminated. But is it possible that this could be just another attempt to persuade us to stop using cash? I said right at the start of this fiasco that one of the hidden aims was to stop us using cash.

The Government is going to give or lend some money to self-employed workers who are in financial distress, and the Chancellor has said that this small generosity will lead to a permanent change in the tax status of the self-employed. In other words, the self-employed will probably have to pay the same National Insurance rate as employed workers – but they will not receive unemployment benefit. The long-term consequences of all this will be far reaching. I pity anyone under 40. Their future becomes grimmer by the day.

A few months ago, the country was divided into two groups. On the one hand there were those who thought that we should leave the EU and strike out on our own. On the other hand there were those who believed that we should remain within the EU. Today, the country is divided again. This time it is divided into those who believe that our leaders are lying and have a hidden agenda, or possibly several hidden agendas, and those who trust our leaders implicitly and who are prepared to dob in anyone who dares to disobey our Dictator.

The death total in Italy is still being used as evidence supporting the UK Government's oppressive policies. But the figures from Italy are wrong. Studies published in the US concluded that as few as 12% of those who allegedly died from the disease may have really died from it. Just because someone has the new disease and dies it is not necessarily correct to conclude that the one was responsible for the other. If someone who has acne is unfortunate enough to die it does not necessarily follow that the acne was the cause of their death.

The media at large seem determined to follow the popular line and sell fear and consternation.

April 2nd 2020

According to figures collected by the European Monitoring of Excess Mortality for Public Health Action, officially recorded figures for Europe show that there have been fewer deaths in 2020 than there were in 2019, 2018 and 2017. Indeed, the death rates for this year are so far substantially lower than they were in any of the last three years. So, either we should have all been locked in our homes in 2019, 2018 and 2017 or else the current hysteria is the biggest piece of social manipulation in modern history.

The UK Government says it wants to manage the incidence of the disease so that hospitals can cope with the millions who will need help. And so they want to keep everyone indoors. It's a sort of reverse of the usual inoculation policy where you inoculate loads of people and that provides herd immunity. The idea of herd immunity is, of course, to protect the community at a cost - the cost being the number of individuals who will be damaged by the stuff from a syringe. The idea now is that by keeping people indoors you slow the spread. Of course, it does mean that when you eventually let people out of their homes they will have no immunity and so, if the Government's theory works, there will be a big spike of cases in the summer and autumn. (This would, of course, be exactly the same with any infection treated in this way.) Then the Government will have a damned good excuse to keep its oppressive new powers and they will expect us to be grateful for any tiny fragment of freedom they toss our way. It's easy to think that our Government is merely exhibiting the usual confusion and incompetence. But it's worse than that. Look at the Emergency Bill that was passed on the 26th March (and that most people still haven't heard of) and it is clear that we are now living in a police state.

The scary news in the UK is that the NHS is having to throw people out of hospital wards because it only has around 142,000 beds. That is a pitifully low number of beds. We have 2.6 hospital beds per 1,000 population (compared to 4.5 on average in other countries). As our population has risen (thanks to unlimited immigration) so the number of beds has fallen. The only thing the NHS leads the world in is administrators. We have few doctors, nurses and beds but we have masses of obscenely highly paid bureaucrats. Astonishingly the number of beds in the NHS has been falling for decades – just as the population has been soaring. Over 40,000 hospital beds were lost during John Major's seven years as Prime Minister. Tony Blair's decade as Prime Minister saw a drop of just under 30,000 in the number of beds available. And the trend has continued since then. Thirty years ago the NHS had 299,000 beds. Today, the NHS has 142,000 beds. At the same time the number of highly paid administrators has increased, and it is fair to say that the number of beds has been decreasing at roughly the inverse rate to which the number of desks has been increasing.

Expert commentators keep saying that the illness caused by the 'crisis' disease cannot be compared to the flu. Why not? They both produce much the same symptoms. They both kill people (usually by causing pneumonia). They can both kill healthy people of all ages but they tend to kill people who are suffering from underlying health problems. The only big difference I can think of is that we don't close down the world economy for the flu. What the devil are we going to do if the plague comes back?

We are still trying to register with Sainsbury's to get groceries delivered. We used to have food from Sainsbury's but now they say they won't deliver unless I prove I am over 70-years-old. I have done this so much I am bored. Once this fiasco is over I intend to boycott Sainsbury's for ever. Antoinette and I went out yesterday and managed to find a rival supermarket which had food for sale so it's pickled beetroot, spaghetti alphabet and pineapple chunks for tea. And I managed to buy hazelnuts for the squirrels so they're happy.

Official figures for February show that (even including the deaths from the new disease) the number of people dying from respiratory disease is lower this year than last year. In the whole of February 2019, there were 7,525 deaths from respiratory disease. In the whole of February 2020, there were 6,262 deaths from respiratory disease. When the media scream about how many have died we must remember that in a bad year the ordinary flu can kill over 600,000 people worldwide. Only by sharing the truth can we overcome the bizarre hysteria which has overtaken the world.

The courts are planning to do away with juries and allow judges to act alone. Gosh. This will doubtless make it much easier for the Government to lock up people who insist on telling the truth. The European Union has long wanted to get rid of juries. They are messy and unpredictable and expensive. You don't have to be paranoid or to believe in conspiracy theories to see what is happening here. How many of these changes will be reversed? My guess is none but it could be less than that.

Dead bodies can now be cremated without a second doctor's certificate. This will make it very easy for the next Dr Harold Shipman to kill thousands without ever being spotted.

The enthusiasm for making sure the number of deaths from the 'crisis' continues to soar is so great that anyone who is decapitated in a motoring accident will, if proven to have the infection, be doubtless listed as a related death. No effort will be spared to maximise the death rate. The average number of deaths caused by flu in England alone in an average sort of year is 17,000 and the authorities will be desperate to get the death total in England to exceed that by the middle of next week.

The police who have been abusing their new powers should be sacked – they have proved that they are incapable of using their powers with good sense and compassion. They won't even be disciplined, of course because we are living in a police state so who is going to discipline them? They should have their truncheons confiscated and hidden in dark and personal places.

I gather that some of those advising the Government are talking about a whole series of lockdowns. (I still prefer the phrase 'house arrest'). These folk are apparently under the misapprehension that it would be possible for businesses to close down for a month, open for a couple of weeks, close for a month and so on ad infinitum. The people who think up such drivel are clearly living in ivory towers far removed from real life as the rest of us know it.

April 3rd 2020

I have been pointing out for ages that testing people is absolutely vital. When a patient is ill you can't start treating them until you have made a diagnosis. In a pandemic you can't start treating the population until you know how many of them have the disease.

Trying to decide how to prevent the spread of any infection is all guesswork if you don't know how many people have it and how many people have had it.

And you cannot possibly know how dangerous a disease is until you know what percentage of those who have it need medical attention and what percentage are dying.

The Government in the UK is currently testing less than 10,000 people a day. The people being tested are mostly the sick who are in hospital. Not even NHS staff are being properly tested.

The population of the UK is around 60,000,000.

If you test 10,000 a day then it will take 6,000 days to test everyone.

That's more than 16 years.

So the UK Government's testing programme will be completed by the year 2036.

And so in 16 years' time we will know what we should (or should not) do.

Brilliant.

Absolutely, bloody brilliant.

By then, of course, we will have all forgotten why we were doing the testing.

A couple of weeks ago I felt quite alone in my views. Now, I don't feel quite so alone. For example, Professor John P.A.Ionannidis, co-director of Stanford University's Meta-Research Innovation Center and professor of medicine, biomedical data science, statistics and epidemiology and population health has described the response as a 'fiasco in the making'. He says that we are making major decisions based on 'utterly unreliable' data. Moreover, he claims that the data which is available suggests that we are likely to be severely overreacting and that the extreme measures being taken may result in unnecessary and catastrophic consequences. He says (as I have frequently argued) that the limited testing means that we are probably missing most of the people who have been infected and that this makes reported fatality rates from the World Health Organisation meaningless. Professor Ionannidis points out that although the fatality rate on the Diamond Princess cruise ship was 1.0%, the population was mostly elderly – the most at risk group. He calculates that the death rate is probably more likely 0.125% with a range between 0.025% and 0.625% and adds that a death rate of 0.05% is lower than the death rate with the ordinary winter flu. Finally, Professor Ionannidis points out that some other similar infections which have been regarded as 'mild' or 'common cold type' have had fatality rates as high as 8% in nursing homes. Other experts agree with Professor Ionannidis.

The UK Government's policy (and the prediction of 500,000 deaths and the most draconian controls on our freedom in history) came from Professor Neil Ferguson and his team at Imperial College London. Professor Ferguson (who appears to be a mathematician and does not seem to have a medical degree) has criticised those (like me) who have compared the new disease to flu. 'It is ludicrous, frankly, to suggest that the severity of this infection is comparable to season flu – ludicrous and dangerous,' he is reported to have said though, as a qualified doctor, I find it difficult to understand why he says this. He criticised Professor Sunetra Gupta and her team who suggested that half the UK's population could have been affected. Professor Gupta's suggestion was also criticised because it hasn't been peer reviewed. But as far as I can see the work done by Imperial College hasn't been peer reviewed either.

Significantly, recent figures from the United States Centers for Disease Control show that during the last few months the flu has infected 38 million Americans, put 390,000 in hospital and killed 23,000. Those are almost certainly massive underestimates. No one seems bothered by these figures because the flu isn't a new disease. As far as I have seen no parts of the mass media have reported this.

It is Ferguson's theories which have led to the lockdown which is causing so much distress. The Government in the UK seems so wedded to Ferguson's theories that I fear that Ministers would acquiesce if he suggested that we should all stand on our heads in buckets of custard. But another academic, Professor Michael Thrusfield of Edinburgh University has pointed out that Ferguson was 'instrumental' for the modelling which led to the cull of more than six million animals during the foot and mouth outbreak in 2001.

Professor Thrusfield, an expert in animal diseases, claimed that the cull was a result of incorrect assumptions and that Imperial's report was 'not fit for purpose' and 'severely flawed'. Professor Ferguson defended Imperial's work on foot and mouth, claiming that they were using 'limited data' at the time. But now, with the 'crisis' infection they are again using limited data.

I will tell you if I was wrong about this 'crisis'. But will Professor Ferguson and the Government tell you if they were wrong?

Meanwhile, there are one or two other significant things happening today.

First, polling from MORI has found that 20% of Britons think it is likely they have already had the disease. Another 14% think it is fairly likely that they have had it. If they are correct then a third of the country has had the disease, had relatively mild symptoms and could be out and about without risk.

Second, the UK now appears to be quoted as giving mortality rate figures for 'people who have died after testing positive'. 'If you died with it then you died of it.' This is exactly what was done in Italy – resulting in a much higher death rate than in other countries. As I have said many times before, people who test positive and who die have not necessarily died because of the infection. They may have died of heart or lung disease. They may have fallen out of bed and cracked their skulls. This is a schoolboy mistake. Or it isn't a mistake at all, but a deliberate attempt to cover up the truth.

Looking at the news about this bizarre fiasco raises far more questions than answers.

Has the Government delayed mass testing because they fear what the tests will show? The Government is going to be vilified if it is proven that the lockdown was unnecessary.

I gather that a new app is being introduced that will enable the authorities to know exactly where you are at all times and, moreover, to know who you have met and for how long and where. George Orwell didn't make that one up.

I read that Imperial College had claimed that the first week of the lockdown saved 370 British lives. Even if this is true (and I don't have the foggiest idea how they can be so sure) I believe that the number of deaths caused by the lockdown far exceeds 370. Many patients have had essential, potentially life-saving surgery delayed. Tests have been delayed. Treatments have been delayed. How many thousands will die as a result? I don't know and nor does anyone else. But if death rates from cancer rise in the next year or two we will know the cause. My guess is that the number who will die as a direct result of the lockdown will be far, far greater than 370. Once again, the cure will be worse than the disease.

The truth is that the new disease will stop being a problem when enough people in the country have immunity. That's the principle behind mass inoculation. But locking people in their homes means that people will not acquire immunity. Once we are allowed out of our homes then the number of infected people will increase. And the lockdown will be reintroduced. This could go on for years. There will doubtless be a spike of infections in the autumn as the weather gets colder.

And talking of bad weather, we are now being told to prepare for blackouts as a result of a shortage of staff at electric companies. Will that be the last straw? The nation will be locked in their homes, with no light, no heat, no hot food or drinks and no television, no computer games and no radio or mobile telephone. Treating the human consequences will require thousands of psychiatrists, psychologists and marriage guidance counsellors.

The fact that should be remembered is that epidemiologists do not have a great track record. They are rather like investment analysts and astrologers in having very patchy results. In 2014, for example, the Centers for Disease Control and Prevention forecast 1.4 million cases of Ebola in West Africa. In the end, the epidemic resulted in less than 30,000 reported cases. In the UK, predictions for deaths from SARS, etc., have been way off the mark. However, even if Professor Ferguson turns out to have been wrong, my guess is that he'll end up with a knighthood or a peerage.

In my first YouTube video I warned that the fiasco would lead to the demonization and abandonment of the elderly. I was mocked and criticised for airing this fear. However, there seems little doubt now that this was entirely accurate and that health services are discriminating against the elderly. Indeed, there have been suggestions that many care home residents will be denied any hospital care – and so death rates will rise. This is discrimination. Imagine the furore if the NHS decided not to treat any other group in society. 'Children to be denied health care'. 'Women to be denied health care'. 'Gays to be denied health care'. The mind boggles.

The truth is that if the Government had done more widespread testing and if that testing had shown that the number of infected people was ten or twenty times as high as is currently being suggested, then the death rate would be one tenth or one twentieth. And that would make the infection far less dangerous. These are not wild assumptions. Indeed, the Government's own chief scientific adviser suggested, when there had been 590 diagnosed cases, that the real figure was 5,000 to 10,000 cases. So that would put the death rate alongside that of flu.

It is constantly worth remembering that on March 19th it was officially decided that the new disease should no longer be classified as a 'high consequence infectious disease'. This downgrade was not published until March 21st. Shortly afterwards, the country was put into lockdown and the 358-page Emergency Bill was published giving the Government and the police extraordinary powers never before seen in Britain.

The Government is in due course almost certain to claim that its lockdown policy has reduced the number of deaths. But this is nonsense because we don't know how many would have died without the lockdown policy. It is perfectly possible that the lockdown policy has made little or no difference to mortality rates from the but I strongly suspect that the lockdown policy has already increased the number of people dying because it has deprived people with other illnesses of normal medical care.

The figures from Italy are constantly being used to frighten us. But the average age of those dying in Italy was 78.5 years. And as I have previously explained, most of the deaths were probably not caused by the specific infection that was put on the death certificates.

In contrast, the authorities in Iceland have been testing their population very enthusiastically and they have found that up to half of infections are almost completely without symptoms. Most of the rest are fairly trivial. In Iceland there have been 648 cases and two deaths – which give a death rate of 0.3 % which is much the same as we would expect from the flu.

I am bewildered by the fact that there has still been very little debate about Professor Ferguson's 'models'. There should be a great debate because if Professor Ferguson is wrong then incalculable damage is being done to whichever countries are following the Imperial College thinking. The Imperial College 'model' should be closely examined and dissected. Has anyone outside Imperial taken a look at it? I'd love to see precisely how Professor Ferguson and his team reached their conclusions. If they are wrong then they must surely take responsibility for the biggest cock up in history. If the Imperial College advice was overly pessimistic, as I believe it was, then Boris Johnson is surely toast. The nation will be damned near destroyed for nothing. Vast numbers of people will have been forced to wait for essential medical treatment. Vast numbers of people will be left unemployed. Vast numbers of businesses will go bust. The education of millions of children will have been savagely disrupted and probably permanently damaged. And, around the world governments have passed legislation taking away almost all our traditional freedoms.

April 4th 2020

According to the BBC, the Brighton and Hove Clinical Commissioning Group (a bunch of NHS managers) have allegedly issued a document telling GPs and nursing homes that vulnerable people may not be admitted to hospital for treatment if they contract the disease. Indeed, one GP apparently told a care home manager that no residents aged over 75 would be admitted to hospital.

It was always going to happen.

The Nazis did it – regarding old folk as worthless and an expensive nuisance. Why bother to feed people who can't put in a good day's work in the salt mines?

Now the NHS wants to kill off the old folk.

Old people who fall over and break limbs will presumably be left to die in pain. Any old person careless enough to have a heart attack will just be left to rot. The old person who stays in bed (to try to keep safe) will probably develop a deep vein thrombosis and die anyway.

I predicted that this would happen when this fiasco started – and was mocked for doing so.

'Oh no, no one would do anything like that,' they said.

I wonder what older MPs think of this? And, remember: a big chunk of the House of Lords is over 75. The only really loveable members of the Royal family are well into the danger area.

It used to be only actresses who lied about their age.

Now, we old folk will all have to lie about our age if we want the NHS to look after us.

I realise that it is, so far, only one part of the NHS which wants to leave the old folk to die. But this will spread if we don't stop it.

If this report is true then the bastards in Brighton and Hove who are responsible for this Nazi-style policy should be named and fired immediately for gross and unforgiveable inhumanity.

This isn't one of those administrative errors that can be forgotten with some sort of mealy mouthed explanation.

No decent society in history has ever treated its old folk this badly.

And what's behind all this hysteria?

It's not the plague.

I'm not the only doctor who believes that the infection causing this 'crisis' is almost certainly nothing more than a jumped up version of the flu with a better marketing strategy.

April 6th 2020

So, we can now be pretty sure that the over 75s are going to be denied medical treatment. The first inklings have appeared. And compulsory inoculation is on its way. I got those two right, I'm afraid.

So, what else is planned as part of the global hoax?

Well, I'd still take a bet that Brexit is finished. I fear that the behind-the-scenes power brokers who opposed Brexit will use this manufactured 'crisis' as an excuse to abandon our leaving the EU. You might expect that big companies would be suing the Government for its handling of the 'crisis'. But most big company bosses are sitting on their wallets because they see this as a last opportunity to sound the death-knell for Brexit. The longer the lockdown lasts the greater the chance that Brexit will be just an almost memory.

Cheques and cash will be gone within a year or two at most. We'll have to use plastic for everything we do. That will give the State complete knowledge about our movements and habits.

And I can pretty well guarantee that the 'temporary' powers the Government has given itself (and the police) will turn out to be permanent. When Governments grab power they tend to hang onto them. As Milton Friedman once observed 'nothing is as permanent as a temporary Government programme'.

If you're in any doubt about the future, read the Government's Emergency Bill which they must have been preparing for some time. It's 358 pages long so they didn't put it together in an afternoon.

Even Lord Sumption, the former Supreme Court Judge, is reported to have talked about 'collective hysteria' and to have used the phrase 'police state'.

The Government can issue orders with no legal check or authority and the police must do what Ministers tell them to do. Pretty much the same is true around the world. Computers, mobile phones and tracking software mean that Governments can now keep track of their citizens 24 hours a day.

The odd thing is, of course, that the Government knows where all pensioners live but, despite having forbidden relatives or friends to visit them, it has deliberately made no effort to ensure that the elderly are receiving food supplies. How many old people will starve to death in the next two months? How many dead bodies will be found behind locked doors?

And the Government must know that the lockdown will result in far, far more deaths than the 'crisis'. Operations and treatment programmes have been 'postponed' though no one knows for how long. People are eating what they can find and getting little or no real exercise. Indeed, unless the Government is comprised entirely of halfwits they must realise that the lockdown will have already killed far more people than the 'crisis'.

But the Government has had it easy so far. The media has built up the 'crisis' with a daily diet of aggressive fear-making. There has been no debate. Although I haven't accepted any of them I've received numerous invitations to appear on radio and TV around the world, but I haven't received any invitations from British media. (If I were talking nonsense it would be easy to take me apart, wouldn't it?)

The constant building up of fear has worked. The majority are enthusiastic about being locked in. They are enthusiastic about inoculation. They are watching far more TV than ever and drinking more booze than ever. The man who used to sit on the top of the Clapham Omnibus is now sat at home growing fat and lazy and obedient. Millennials are filled with a terror that they cannot deal with. Zombie companies which were about to go bust will be saved with taxpayers' money. And yet taxpayers know that within a year they will be paying the highest ever rates of tax and who would bet against VAT rising to 25% or more?

It has long been clear to anyone who doesn't leave a slimy trail when they move about, that this fiasco is either the biggest cock up in world history or the result of a conspiracy. But any suspicion that the Government could have simply made a series of mistakes has long gone. This has the fingerprints of the Bilderbergers over every inch. And everywhere I look I see new signs of Orwellian horrors. Those who are puzzled by the fact that the disease appears to have been dealt with quickly and relatively easily in China should know that the Bilderbergers almost certainly have no power in China. Oddly, the new disease appears to be a real menace only in those countries where the Bilderbergers hold sway.

Everywhere I look I am alarmed.

The Emergency Bill gives doctors the right to certify individuals insane and have them carted away without objection.

And there is evidence that some pathologists have apparently decreed that dead patients who have the disease must now be cremated without examination. I've seen a briefing which states: 'If a death is believed to be due to confirmed… infection there is unlikely to be any need for a post-mortem examination to be conducted and the Medical Certificate of Cause of Death should be issued'. The key word here is surely 'believed'. Surely, this is a murderer's charter? The wise murderer will merely insist that his victim had a cough. The body will then be burned without examination. And, as a dear friend points out, what about other causes of death that might be missed? We could miss an outbreak of the plague.

Knowing that nowhere near enough people are dying to justify the oppressive new measures they've introduced, the authorities are quietly making sure that most of the people who die are classified as related deaths. Indeed, there is some evidence that people are being classified as victims without ever having been tested. I'll take a bet that non-related deaths will fall noticeably as a result. Deaths from heart disease and cancer will mysteriously drop as everyone who dies is classified wrongly. It seems that we are doing what the Italians did – if a patient has the infection and they die then they died of the infection. But I suspect we're going one step further. If someone who dies is thought to have had the infection, or might have had the infection, then they are victims and their death is added to the total. The lack of testing makes this easy.

The sad thing is that at the end of it, whenever that finally comes, Boris, our brave leader, and Ferguson, the mathematical modeller whose disputed work led to the death of six million animals during the foot and mouth 'crisis', will stand side by side and announce, with surprising humility, that they saved us all.

And I fear that most people, staunch believers, will give grateful thanks and applaud their saviours. They will consider the price they've had to pay, the loss of their freedom, acceptably small.

April 13th 2020

Right at the beginning of the affair I pointed out that according to the World Health Organisation, the ordinary flu kills between 250,000 and 600,000 people a year – most of them in the winter months. I said that if the new disease hadn't killed between 100,000 and 150,000 people around the world by the middle of April then it would be clear that it was not as dangerous as we had been told and, indeed, not as dangerous as the flu.

Well, the authorities are claiming that the death total has now reached 100,000.

So is the 'crisis' disease as deadly as the mathematicians and the politicians said it was?

No – because they have fiddled the figures.

As I pointed out earlier, anyone who has the new infection, or is thought to have it even though they have not been tested, will be put down as having died of it. Time and time again, the authorities report that someone died 'with' the disease. Not 'of' the disease.

So, if you fall downstairs and break your neck, but you had a cough before you died, then you will be classified as a 'crisis' death. Honest. I'm not kidding. If you had a heart attack but were thought to have the new infection then you officially died of the infection rather than the heart attack. A lack of widespread testing makes this possible. And post mortems have been abandoned for many patients. All this means that the numbers have been wildly exaggerated.

Remember, I pointed out that in Italy it has been established that only around 12% of the people listed as having died of the new infection were really killed by it. The other 88% almost certainly died of something else. (The Italian Government's scientific advisor reported that anyone who dies in Italy and who has the infection will be listed as having died of it. The National Institute of Health revaluated the death certificates and concluded that only 12% showed a direct causality.)

And in the UK, Imperial College (which originally forecast the disease would kill 500,000 people) has admitted that two thirds of the people who have been listed as having died of the 'crisis' would have died anyway – of something else.

I have no doubt that the figures have been distorted in the same way in other countries.

So the total worldwide number of deaths is, at most, probably between a quarter and a third of the alleged current total – that is it may be between 25,000 and 33,000 but is probably considerably lower.

And that makes the 'crisis' disease far less deadly than a mild strain of the flu. It is certainly absurd to compare it to the plague as has frequently been done by hysterical commentators. The plague killed 40% of the population when it swept through Europe. And to compare the 'crisis' to the Second World War is an insult to those soldiers and civilians who lived through those terrible years.

Fiddling the figures is the final, cruel deceit – to sustain the fear.

Meanwhile, it is now widely acknowledged that, as I wrote some time ago on the number of people who have died as a direct result of the restrictions brought in by governments will far exceed the number of people who will die as a result of the 'crisis'.

The British Government has now admitted that the side effects of the 'cure' (the lockdowns and so on) will result in 150,000 unnecessary deaths. On 30th March I suggested on www.vernoncoleman.com that the unnecessary death figure would be 100,000 to 250,000. No one is now suggesting that there will be anywhere near that number of deaths from the 'crisis' in the UK.

A senior NHS official has expressed 'concern' that sick children are not being treated because of the lockdown 'cure'.

And the United Nations estimates that worldwide 25 million jobs will be lost as a result of the cure for the 'crisis'. Some claim the figure could be as high as 190 million. Actually, virtually no jobs will be lost because of the 'crisis'. It's the lockdowns, the cure for the 'crisis', which will cause the job losses. Once again, I predicted that this would happen weeks ago.

Every fact I have provided has been absolutely accurate. Every prediction I've made has been proven accurate.

But even if they wanted to do so, the scientists, the politicians and the media are now wedded to this deceit. Even if they wanted to, how could they possibly admit that they got it all so very, very wrong?

But there is another danger that no one seems to have noticed.

By exaggerating the number of deaths the authorities are endangering us all. You cannot investigate a disease when you don't keep proper records. As the weeks pass by we should be able to learn a good deal about this disease. But we won't be able to do any useful research because we don't know who really died from it and who died from something else. We can't work out whether the disease mostly affects people who are meat eaters, or who have been inoculated against the flu or who have red hair because the information we have is inaccurate and useless. For example, I have spotted that this disease seems to affect Asians a good deal. Is that observation supported by the facts?

Today, I heard from a doctor in Australia who is asking colleagues to help find out if the infection is more (or less) likely to affect those individuals who were inoculated against the flu. We'll never be able to answer that question because we don't really know which of the 'victims' really died of the 'crisis' infection.

And this evening I saw that it has been reported Matt Hancock, the Health Secretary, says that the NHS has 2,295 empty intensive care beds. The average number of empty intensive care beds before the 'crisis' was 800. So, the NHS has 1,495 more empty intensive care beds during the 'crisis' than it had before the so-called 'crisis' began. And the *Financial Times* has apparently reported that almost half the beds in some English hospitals are lying empty. It has been widely reported that the massive new hospitals which had been built at enormous public expense are virtually empty of patients and would obviously remain so. The number of empty beds in British hospitals was four times the usual number at this time of year. It is clearly not true that the NHS is overrun. Hancock, the Health Secretary, should resign.

April 14th 2020

There was one simple thing governments could (and should) have done: random testing of people outside hospitals.

If they had done that they would have known how many people had the infection, how many people were unaffected by it and how many people were made ill by it. They would have also known the true mortality rate. And they would not have had to rely on a 'mathematical model' which originally estimated that 500,000 people would die in the UK but which eventually brought that down to well under 20,000.

Random tests of just 10,000 people in various communities in each nation would have provided valuable information. The testing should have included people of different ages. It should have included some people who were ill and who were well.

So why the devil didn't they do that?

Pollsters can get good results from asking questions of a good number of people. So why didn't governments everywhere do tests in cities, towns and villages? The information obtained would have been invaluable – and would have probably enabled governments to avoid deadly and damaging lockdowns. Those countries which did some testing benefitted enormously from the knowledge.

There are two explanations for why governments didn't do these tests:

They didn't think of it. (The cock up theory.)

They didn't want to do it because they wanted to turn democracies into dictatorships. (The conspiracy theory.)

I can think of no other explanation.

(The unavailability of tests is no explanation. There seem to have been plenty of tests available for celebrities and footballers.)

I have just been sent a reference for a study in the J. Clin Microbiol which suggests that recent flu inoculation can give rise to antibody testing as positive and suggests 'routine inoculation as a potential cause of false-positive antibody test results'. I hope scientific advisors around the world are aware of this.

April 15ᵗʰ 2020

It's illuminating to think back to the days before the panic began.

In France, the yellow vest riots were still in full flow. President Macron had pretty much lost control of his country.

In Hong Kong, the demonstrators were causing mayhem and the Chinese Government was facing serious problems.

All over the world, protestors were causing chaos with demonstrations inspired by climate change campaigners.

In Europe there were increasing tensions as countries such as Italy and Greece struggled with a currency that was too strong for them. The German people were becoming very tetchy about the future cost of supporting the European Union.

And the issues over Brexit were still causing serious concern among hard-line Remainers – who were still hoping to overturn the democratic will of the British people.

In the United States, the ideological battles were heightened as the Presidential election got underway.

The world was, in short, in rare turmoil.

Today, the world is pretty much one big police state.

Demonstrations of any kind are outlawed. Public meetings are outlawed. Elections have been cancelled.

And there is now talk that social distancing will have to be indefinite. Researchers talk of a need for more surveillance.

Convenient, eh?

Mass testing would show whether or not the lockdown was necessary. The financial cost would be incredibly small. But very little testing is going on. Why could that be? One would almost be tempted to think that the authorities don't want to know whether lockdowns are necessary.

16th April 2020

Right from the start of this 'crisis' I have been no great fan of Neil Ferguson, who is professor of mathematical biology at Imperial College, London. My doubts about his ability to guide us through the 'crisis' have built quite rapidly during the last few weeks.

Ferguson appears to be the man behind government policy. He believes that social distancing must be maintained indefinitely. And when he warns, the Government listens.

But look at his track record as summarised by Steerpike on *The Spectator* website.

In 2001, the Imperial team did the modelling on foot and mouth disease which led to a cull of six million sheep, pigs and cattle. The cost to the UK was around £10 billion. But the Imperial's work has been described as 'severely flawed'. In 2002, Ferguson predicted that up to 50,000 people would die from mad cow disease. He said that could rise to 150,000 if sheep were involved. In the UK, the death total was 177. In 2005, Ferguson said that up to 200 million people could be killed by bird flu. The total number of deaths was 282 worldwide. In 2009, Ferguson and his chums at Imperial advised the Government which, relying on that advice, said that swine flu would kill 65,000 people in the UK. In the end, swine flu killed 457 people in the UK.

Finally, Ferguson has admitted that his model is based on undocumented 13-year-old computer code intended for use with an influenza epidemic.

No one seems to have questioned Ferguson's work— despite the fact that if he is wrong again (which I believe he is) the nation will be pushed back into the Dark Ages as a result of his work.

My critics (and there are a great many of them) might like to look at the list of accurate warnings and predictions I have made in the years gone by. The list is taken from my book, *How To Stop Your Doctor Killing You*, which was first published in 1996, and the list appears on the second page of my website.

I was the first author to write about the excessive power of the drug companies – in my book, *The Medicine Men* in 1975. I was the only doctor to rightly judge that the Government's warnings on AIDS were wild exaggerations. (My views were summarised in my book, *The Health Scandal* in 1988. In the same book I warned about the huge demographic problems facing many Western countries but particularly the UK.) Naturally, I was vilified for that advice. I was the first doctor to warn that stress could cause massive harm to the human body, in my book, *Stress Control* in 1977. I was the first doctor to warn about the dangers of benzodiazepines, in a series of articles and TV programmes in the 1970s and 1980s, and in my book, *Life Without Tranquillisers* (1985). I was vilified for that, though the Government eventually admitted that I was right and that they had changed their guidelines to doctors because of my articles. I was the first doctor to warn about the association between eating meat and cancer. (In my book, *Food for Thought* which was first published in 1994.) And so on and so on. I don't think I am being immodest when I point out that my track record is a damned sight better than Ferguson's.

I find it difficult to understand why the Government is following Ferguson's advice.

Are our ministers really as incompetent as they seem? Or is there some ulterior motive? Is it a cockup or a conspiracy?

We have to go to the pharmacy, the bank and the supermarket tomorrow and neither of us is looking forward to it. Antoinette and I are both natural recluses and since we have been out of our home no more than three times in the last month, our reclusiveness is growing. There is a real danger that we (and thousands of others) will find it nigh on impossible to leave the house at all if the lockdown goes on for much longer. This mass house arrest is going to cause massive mental problems as well as huge physical ones. Suicides, depression, domestic violence and murders will all rise – probably quite dramatically. I don't think that the people who thought up the idea of lockdown thought through the idea, and I suspect that they still have absolutely no idea of the damage they have done. The serious mental health problems created by the lockdown are going to be with us for many years to come. There aren't anywhere enough psychiatrists and psychologists to deal with the people who will need help. My big fear is that doctors will simply hand out lorry loads of anxiolytics and antidepressants when these will merely make things worse and ensure they last eternally.

Today, I saw the deaths registered by the ONS for the last but one full week in March. There were 10,645 deaths in England and Wales. That compares with a five year average for similar weeks of

10,573. That hardly seems justification for closing down the country and causing 150,000 deaths. (That is the Government's own estimate of the number of deaths the lockdown will cause.)

I would love to debate live on TV or radio with Ferguson. They would never allow it to happen, of course.

Why not?

I believe my credentials are as good as those of any of the people interviewing him.

I was the first doctor to question the 'crisis'. I have the best track record around for making judgements about health crises. I'm a *Sunday Times* bestselling author. One of my novels was turned into a £14 million award winning movie. I've written columns for four national newspapers (three of the columns lasted for a decade each). I've presented TV programmes on both BBC and ITV. I was the original breakfast TV doctor. And I was a GP principal for ten years.

During the last month or so I have received a large number of interview requests from TV and radio companies around the world but I have not received any invitations at all from UK based broadcasters.

Strange.

April 17th

A few weeks ago, my website (which has been on the internet for over 25 years) suddenly disappeared from Google.

I have no idea what Facebook looks like. I've never even visited the site. But the other day I decided to drag myself a little further into the 21st century by joining Facebook.

So I filled in a few of those little boxes and waited.

And I then received a reply telling me that I could not join because of the need to protect the Facebook community.

So why, I wonder, does Facebook feel the need to protect its community from the truth? Why are Mr Zuckerberg and his chums fearful of letting a 73-year-old author onto their site?

All I do is tell the truth and then give my perfectly legal conclusions.

So which truths do they think may harm the Facebook community?

Or is it just the truth in general which is unacceptable?

I have no idea though I suspect that someone at Facebook disapproves of my telling the bald truth about the 'crisis'.

Still, if you are on Facebook it will no doubt be nice for you to know that you are being protected from me. I rather think that Facebook and its fellows should be known as anti-social media.

And a variety of assorted and unacceptable truths

Today, my three videos for YouTube suddenly disappeared into a black hole. They have become almost impossible to find, and it seemed to me that for much of the day the views which I was told they were getting, simply weren't being registered. Curious.

April 18th

A doctor working in an intensive care unit is quoted as wondering where all the usual patients had gone to. (The beds which were occupied were occupied only by patients who had the 'crisis' infection or who were thought to have it.) He said he couldn't understand where the stroke victims, heart attack patients and so on had gone to.

Well, I can tell him. They had all been abandoned. Most of them are doubtless at home. A good number will probably die there.

One of the most disappointing aspects of the fiasco is the way the medical profession has allowed itself to get dragged along in the hysteria. Doctors should be screaming about the way patients with cancer and other deadly diseases are being side-lined and abandoned. But the medical and nursing professions seem to be enjoying their hero status far too much to worry about the way health care seems to be obsessed with a single disease – that will turn out to be no more deadly than a fairly standard influenza. Hospital bosses shouldn't be clapped – but they should be clapped in irons for failing to speak up to protect the most vulnerable. I hate to say it but we should be booing not clapping the people who made the decision to close hospitals to cancer patients.

Tonight, I was delighted to see an eminent Swedish epidemiologist agreeing with the arguments I put forward six weeks ago. Professor Giesecke was the first Chief Scientist of the European Centre for Disease Prevention and Control and an advisor to the

World Health Organisation's director general. He agrees with my point that locking people up delays the development of herd immunity and agrees with my original belief that the Imperial College modelling was never worth the attention it received. Professor Johan Giesecke said he had never seen an unpublished non-peer-reviewed paper have so much impact on government policy. He estimates that the fatality rate of the 'crisis' infection will be similar to that of the flu – something in the region of 0.1%. He describes the 'crisis' infection as a 'mild disease', similar to the flu.

And so, here is yet another expert agreeing that our lives are being wrecked on the sole basis of a theory from a bloke with an appalling track record. What the devil were the Chief Medical Officer and Chief Scientific Advisor doing to allow this to happen?

I get the feeling that our leaders, and their advisors, all drank an ample serving of Kool-Aid according to the Jim Jones recipe.

But the twist is that we are the ones who are suffering.

Meanwhile, the latest official UK figures show that the total number of deaths is much the same as it always is at this time of the year. Just because everything (heart attack, cancer, flu, varicose veins, rabies, tuberculosis, you-name-it) is being listed as a related death hasn't made any difference to the total. And before Ferguson et al claim that the absence of any rise in deaths is due to their advice, I would like to point out that those countries which have no lockdown appear to have much lower mortality rates than those which do.

The most idiotic news of the last two months is that a good many old people in care homes have died recently.

I wish the journalists who blasted this non-news on their front pages would look at the mortality figures for the elderly. Sadly, that would require a little independent research, and journalists today seem to prefer to print government press releases without questioning them. The sad fact is that old people do commonly die.

In today's *Spectator* magazine, Charles Moore writes about an elderly neighbour of his who is self-isolating. She has twice been telephoned by medical authorities. On both occasions the woman was asked if she was happy to agree not to be resuscitated if she became ill.

April 19th

The bewildering lunacy continues.

So, now the Government says that the over 70s will have to remain under house arrest until at least the autumn of 2022. And even then the over 70s will only be allowed out of their homes if an inoculation is available. To me it seems that the implication is that individuals will be forced to remain under house arrest (and, again, let's stop mincing words – locking people in is house arrest) unless they agree to have the damned inoculation. Those who watched my first YouTube video on March 18th will know that I predicted from the beginning that this whole farce was about demonising the elderly and forcing through a tough inoculation programme.

I feel a huge, billowing sense of blackening despair.

For many over 70s, who let us be blunt the years ahead are not endless, this is a life sentence. They will never be allowed out of their homes again. They will never see friends or relatives except at a distance or via a camera and a screen. They won't be able to visit a solicitor to make a will. They will never be allowed to move house. They will never be able to buy Christmas or birthday cards. They will never be allowed to buy presents for those they love unless they shop online. They will never be allowed to go to a café or a restaurant. They will never be allowed to play sport (and many over 70s enjoy golf, tennis, bowls and other games). They will never again be able to visit a garden centre, a stately home or a wildlife park. Those who run businesses will have to let their businesses die. They will never again be allowed to go on holiday. (Those businesses which rely on attracting the over 70s will quickly go bust.) They won't be able to visit friends or relatives in hospital. They won't be able to go to the pub or the funfair. No more parties.

In short, the over 70s will never again do any of the many things which added spice and flavour to life.

Their homes will forever remain unpainted, steadily falling into disrepair because they are neither allowed to purchase what they need or to hire workmen to visit their homes.

What about those over 70-year-olds who have second homes, in this country or abroad? What about the dozens of MPs who are over 70? (The one good thing to come out of this will be that the House of

Lords will have to close its doors.) What about all those company directors and chairmen who will have to resign?

This is all, typically ill-thought out lunacy because many over 70s are fitter and healthier than folk who are decades younger.

But that's the whole point isn't it?

This is nothing to do with protecting the over 70s.

This is, as I said at the beginning of this unscientific charade, all about oppressing, isolating and excluding the elderly from society.

If the long-term house arrest were being introduced to protect the over 70s, surely they would get some choice in the matter?

The over 70s have already been told that their age makes them ineligible for the health care they have paid for, so why aren't they allowed to take their chances out in the world?

(Has no one else realised that by keeping millions of people under long-term house arrest the Government will be ensuring that those individuals will be particularly susceptible to a whole range of diseases when or if they are eventually allowed out into the community. Moreover, the population will never acquire herd immunity if people are locked away in solitary confinement. This basic error will help to perpetuate the problem and therefore, apparently vindicate the official policy.)

But none of this is about protecting the over 70s. It's all about excluding them from society.

Of course, there are one or two ways around this cruel policy.

Unless and until they are forced to carry their birth certificates with them, oldies will be able to sneak out of their homes (if they can get past the neighbours) as long as they don't look over 70.

Maybe plastic surgery would be an option.

Or, come to think about it, the over 70s could merely change their age.

Today, everyone has the right to decide whether they are male or female.

So, we must all have the right to decide how old we are.

Well, I've decided that I'm now 63. And that's the age I'm going to remain.

I'm no longer in the over 70s age group.

I feel much livelier already.

And what the hell can the bastards do if they catch me sitting in a café with my wife?

Arrest me?

They've done that already.

April 20th

I found Antoinette crying today. It takes a lot to make her cry but she is in a great deal of pain from the scarring and nerve pain caused by her surgery and radiotherapy for breast cancer. The physiotherapist who works at the local hospital wants to help but she is not allowed to see Antoinette and has been sent home because the hospital is pretty well closed. And so the suffering goes on. The physiotherapist did email some exercises for Antoinette to do herself. I wonder if hospitals are emailing details of how to perform your own brain surgery with a fish slice and a soup spoon. Or, maybe, how to build your own radiotherapy machine using a toaster and a hairdryer.

Yesterday, the UK's Health Secretary, Matt Hancock, warned that cancer treatment has come to a juddering halt.

Hancock said that the number of patients visiting their GPs with cancer symptoms was dropping sharply. Referrals by GPs for suspected cancer fell by up to 70% last month.

And whose fault is that?

It's partly the Government's fault for putting all its energy into dealing with the flu bug.

But it is also the fault of the medical profession which is too busy slapping itself on the back for its courage in doing its job to give a damn about the fact that health care in the UK is now a pitiful joke.

There are two stories in the papers today which show just how incompetently the Government is handling its created 'crisis'.

First, the Government has admitted that 100,000 people are flying into Britain each week. No screening is done to see if they are bringing the allegedly lethal infection with them. This would make no sense if the Government's claim that this is a major 'crisis' were true. The official policy seems to be that the Government might consider thinking about testing and isolating people coming into the country at some time in the future.

Second, a scientist working for the Government has said that staff employed to analyse tests have so little work to do that they are being sent home at noon. Working in a laboratory capable of analysing 30,000 samples a day, the scientist said they had processed just 1,000 samples in a day. Hancock, the Health Secretary who claimed that we would be testing huge swathes of the population – at one point the Government promised that we would be testing 100,000 people a day – should be embarrassed. However, I doubt if that is a quality found much among ministers these days.

Finally, I have seen a number of anecdotal reports from emergency room doctors reporting that their hospitals are surprisingly quiet. It has even been reported that in the UK the so-called 'crisis' peaked some time ago, before the widespread house arrest began.

I find it increasingly difficult to believe that this whole damaging exercise in cruelty was not planned. (Remember that 358-page Emergency Bill which appeared overnight?)

The only question is: what was it all for?

April 21st

Matt Hancock the Health Secretary has announced that the British Government is considering passing legislation to make it illegal to criticise inoculation online. Anyone who criticises inoculation will be classified as a terrorist. Telling the truth about inoculation will become an illegal act. It seems reasonable to assume that the same legislation will cover print and other media. I suspect that the Emergency Bill which was passed last month gives the Government the right to do this without any parliamentary discussion.

So, that is the end of free speech in Britain. The Government is now less than an inch away from burning books which contain material which the authorities consider to be unacceptable. Indeed, by targeting the internet, the Government could be described as merely burning books the 21st century way. I know now that if and when this legislation is passed (and I don't think there is any doubt that it will be) and I write about inoculation on my website then I will probably be arrested as a terrorist and my website will be taken down (and used in evidence against me).

Now, wasn't there another government which kept itself warm by doing a little book burning?

I have in the past challenged Government ministers and the Government's Chief Medical Officer to debate the subject of inoculation with me.

Sadly, the challenges have never been accepted. And now there can never be any debate because it would be illegal for me (or anyone else) to criticise inoculation. The philosophy, so prevalent in British universities, of banning speakers who have views which are considered unacceptable has, it seems, become Government policy and will shortly become the law.

'You aren't allowed to say that because I don't agree with it,' is a long stride down the short road to totalitarianism.

As I have already explained, this happened to me in China where all my books in Mandarin were withdrawn from sale after I wrote a column for a Chinese newspaper in which I criticised inoculation.

I thought that was a terrible thing to happen but I never, ever thought it would happen in Britain.

April 22nd

In the UK, figures for the week up to the 10th April showed that deaths from causes other than the 'crisis' disease had risen by several thousand, showing that the lockdown was already having a significant impact on health and mortality figures. We will never know how many people died unnecessarily because the health services were concentrating almost exclusively on the 'crisis' but when the figures are finally added up I believe it will be clear that the Government's own estimate that the lockdown would cause 150,000 unnecessary deaths will be a considerable under-estimate.

According to Cancer Research UK, a reduction in the amount of screening being done means that every week approximately 2,700 people with cancer are not being diagnosed.

Worse still, surgery, radiotherapy and drug treatment have all been cancelled for patients who have been diagnosed. Patients who have been diagnosed with cancer are left in limbo waiting to see what happens next. Screening programmes have been virtually abandoned as all effort is put into dealing with the 'crisis'. According to Cancer Research UK, 200,000 people a week are no longer being screened for bowel, breast and cervical cancer. No one will ever know how many cancers were missed as a result.

Scarily, surveys have shown that the majority of Britons with a view on the matter are happy to continue under house arrest and do not think that the Government need publish any sort of exit strategy.

The campaign to induce a sense of terror has clearly been very successful.

Either the majority of British people are unaware of the facts.

Or they are happy to remain off work and content to receive 80% of their usual income as a payment from the Government.

The longer the lockdown continues, of course, the more reluctant people will be to go back to work. And the more difficult they will find it to get back to what used to be considered 'normal' life. It is now difficult to estimate the size of the Government's eventual debt.

Part Three: My Guide to Our Future

Brexit

If there is any Brexit at all, it will probably be a weakened, watered down version of the one we were promised. The excuse, of course, will be that there has not been time to conduct negotiations. I find it difficult not to suspect that the elderly are being punished by the authorities for being largely responsible for our leaving the European Union. I realise that this sounds rather paranoid but the way our life has changed in the last couple of months means that even the most unlikely scenario must be considered. Who, in January, would have contemplated a world in which huge swathes of the population would be kept under house arrest without there being any solid scientific evidence for doing so?

Cash

We will become a cashless society far sooner than expected. Cheques and currency notes will disappear quickly. Forcing people to use plastic for everything they buy will enable governments to keep a close eye on their citizens. Before last Christmas, there were widespread demands to get rid of cash. The demands came from the big banks (which find cash rather annoying and expensive to handle) and politicians who want to control their populations. It was pointed out that cash provided people with privacy. It was also pointed out that millions of people do not have access to the internet and, therefore, rely on cash. All this has now changed. I suspect that there is nothing any of us can do about this. Even before the 'crisis' arrived to scare everyone silly, there were a number of shops which refused to accept cash. Today, far more shops insist on being paid with plastic. The 'crisis' will have helped banks, governments and shops get rid of cash and they will all be utterly delighted.

Community Life and Leisure Activities

Politicians have said that 'social distancing' will need to be permanent to prevent the spread of infections in the future. This will mean that there will be very few or no cafés, restaurants, theatres or cinemas. If these places stay open they will be forced to keep patrons far apart. The inevitable result of that will be to force prices skywards. (If your restaurant can service 12 diners then the prices will obviously have to be higher than they were when your restaurant serviced 48 diners.) And since most people will be impoverished, it is a safe bet that the majority of eating and drinking establishments will struggle to survive. Pubs are going to close at an even faster rate than in the past because their customers have discovered the job of cheap supermarket beer. Parties will be rare because of the need to obey social distancing rules. When parties are held, the police will insist upon the right to check that the rules are being followed. Nightclubs do not appear to have any sort of future.

Many hairdressing establishments will fail to reopen when the 'crisis' ends. Before the 'crisis', there were 30,000 nail parlours or bars in the United Kingdom. As the nation struggles with poverty and unemployment, many of these will have to close. There will, of course, be far less need to have your hair and nails done when there are no parties, dinners or other events to attend.

Courts

During the 'crisis', courts sat without juries. It is not impossible that this could continue indefinitely. It will be cheaper and it will save time, and compliant judges will doubtless be able to keep politicians satisfied with their decisions.

Demonstrations

By and large, public meetings will be outlawed. In the future, only those demonstrations which are accepted as 'politically correct' will be allowed and even then social distancing guidelines will have to be observed. So, for example, demonstrations about global warming will probably be allowed (since they are 'politically correct') but demonstrations about animal abuses such as vivisection will not. The social distancing rules will take all the spontaneity out of demonstrations so there will be little demand for them.

Education

Only 2% of British children attended physical schools during the lockdown and only a third of those who did not attend school took part in the online lessons which were provided. (When broken down, the figures are even more disturbing since they show that over 50% of pupils from private schools accessed online lessons whereas around 20% of pupils from state schools bothered to do so. The Government expected that around 20% of pupils would attend school (children of parents with essential jobs were entitled to go to school) but the numbers obviously fell considerably short of this. I suspect that these figures have been repeated in other countries. Exams have been cancelled and teachers given the power to decide who 'passed' which exams and who 'failed'. All this was despite the fact that some experts had concluded that closing schools really made no difference to the spread of the disease but would cause massive and entirely economic disruption. Allowing teachers to take the place of examinations will inevitably mean that students who sucked up to their teachers will get good grades, and troublesome students (the ones who usually turn out to be creative and inventive) will suffer. We can expect educational skills to fall dramatically in the future. The incidence of illiteracy and innumeracy will grow. Children from poorer families will suffer most. The effect on society will be dramatic and long-lasting.

A former chief schools inspector, Sir Michael Wilshaw, has stated that some school pupils might have lost out so much because of the lockdown that they will need to repeat the whole year.

As always, these days, I found myself wondering what the hidden agenda might be. There is no doubt that chunks of a population which remain uneducated and ignorant are much easier to control. They are less questioning and far more obedient.

Added to all the other problems will be the nervousness and uncertainty of children of all ages who will feel disturbed and ill at ease as a result of the house arrest policy. Children always feel nervous when going back to school after the long summer holiday but this will be many times worse. Children will find it difficult to settle into classroom life. There will probably be a good deal of misbehaviour and truancy.

A study conducted in Norway showed that the educational damage can be permanent. It appears that every week of absence from school can permanently affect life changes and earning potential.

Teaching unions are demanding to be equipped with gowns and masks before schools can reopen but if this is a serious demand then it is likely that schools will remain closed for months.

A report recently published in the journal *Clinical Infectious Diseases* traced a child who had tested positive and found that although he came into contact with 170 people, he did not transmit the disease to any of them. Was it ever necessary to close schools or was that just another example of the teenage-style hysteria which has overtaken politicians?

Elderly

The elderly had a very bad 'crisis'. And for them the future is now very bleak. Government ministers are talking about keeping the over 70s under house-arrest indefinitely. This will mean that those over 70 will never be allowed to see friends or relatives, to go to work, to engage in sports or hobbies, to take vacations or even to celebrate birthdays and anniversaries.

Most significantly of all, many old people will find that they are denied medical care.

Since I am over 70, I know that if I were to catch the 'crisis' infection, or were to catch some other infection which appeared to be the 'crisis' infection or were to develop symptoms (such as a cough) which suggested that I might possibly have the 'crisis' infection, then I would probably be on my own. (Well, I wouldn't be on my own, of course, because Antoinette would be here with me.) Some NHS administrators have made it pretty clear that there's a chance that no hospital would treat me. And, if I'm out of luck, then quite probably, no GP would treat me either.

It seems that anyone over 70 is too old to be treated by the NHS. (I hate to mention it but no one seems to care that it was the taxes paid by the over 70s which have kept the NHS alive for decades.)

Private hospitals offer no alternative because they don't treat emergencies and, even if they did, they wouldn't be able to treat me because all their beds have been rented by the NHS in case the NHS runs out of beds. (Though judging by the fact that the new hospitals they are building are virtually empty, this seems extremely unlikely. Beds are empty but they're not available to me).

Anyway, if I become part of the 'crisis', or appear to be part of the 'crisis', then I will either die or live. And the only professional help we'll be able to call for will be the undertaker.

(In a clever twist on Catch 22, if you are over 70 then, whatever else you have got wrong with you, you will also officially be deemed to be part of the 'crisis' – whether or not you've been tested and whether or not you show any symptoms. So, since you are officially part of the 'crisis' you will not be entitled to be treated and if/when you die, you will be added to the statistics to make the Governmental policies all that much more acceptable to the masses. I do hope you don't think I am joking because I'm not. Joseph Heller would be proud of whoever thought this one up.)

For the older citizen, life is now a bit like a tightrope walk without a safety net.

If I fall in the garden and break my arm then there's a chance that I'm not going to be treated. The hospitals are apparently too busy waiting for the young patients who might or might not turn up. If I have a retinal detachment then I'll just have to put up with it. If I have chest pains then it'll be two aspirin and wait and see what happens.

The prediction I made less than two months ago was absolutely accurate: the hysteria has turned the elderly into second class citizens. Or, more accurately, into non-citizens.

And so these are worrying times to be old.

It's just another side effect of the Government's hysterical over-reaction.

Those who applaud this state of affairs (and I am afraid there are many who do) might like to reflect upon the fact that one day they too will celebrate their 70th birthday and then suddenly wonder about what lies beyond. And, of course, 60 will soon be the new 70.

Employment

Millions of jobs are going to be lost as companies go bankrupt. Unemployment is going to reach massive and possibly unprecedented levels. One estimate for the UK is that unemployment will reach 6.5 million. This is probably an under-estimate, though the final figure depends upon how long the Government persists with its lockdown policy. There will be some new companies arising out of the ashes (sometimes taking advantage of the wreckage of former companies to buy property, machinery and stock at knock down prices) but they will remain small for years as they struggle to raise capital. When unemployment rises, so does poverty and when poverty increases so do ill health and early death. The consequences of the 'crisis' will be with us for decades to come. Many people will find that skills they acquired in the days before the 'crisis' will be worthless – not simply because of automation but because whole industries will shrink or disappear. (If you have skills as a wine waiter, for example, you will have little opportunity to use those skills if there are few or no restaurants still in business.) And there will be millions who will find going back to work, and fitting again into a routine, incredibly difficult to do. Many people find it hard to go back to work after a fortnight's holiday. Imagine how much more difficult it will be to go back to work after many weeks of rising at 9.30 a.m. and spending the day pottering around the house. The mass house arrest of millions of workers will lead to a population of people who find it difficult to settle into work and who may prefer to adopt an unemployed lifestyle. I wonder if the politicians and their advisors factored this problem into their equation. I rather doubt it.

Epidemiology

Pathologists stopped performing post mortems on patients who may have had the disease involved in the 'crisis' on the grounds that the infection is more dangerous than rabies, tuberculosis or, indeed, any other infection known to man. The result of this controversial and, I believe, unprecedented decision will be that we will, in future, know far less about what people are dying of and why. I fear the number of autopsies performed will never go back to what it had been before the 'crisis'. (Improvements which are introduced during an emergency are always short lived. Changes which are introduced but which damage services to the people are always maintained indefinitely.) In future we will have to rely on mathematicians – such as those who recently advised government. Epidemiologists and mathematical modellers do not have a good track record when it comes to predicting health problems. Just look at the history of Neil Ferguson and Imperial College in the UK for proof of this. The result will be that public health care will, in future, be managed blindfold.

There will doubtless be far more unnecessary scares in the years to come, and we have to retain a mixture of common sense and scepticism when confronted with Government inspired scare stories. The aim of the scare stories is, of course, to maintain a high level of fear. It is much easier to control a population when most of them are fearful. The effectiveness of this approach in the UK can be seen from the fact that the majority of people support the mass house arrests and the police control. Indeed, a majority of the population seems to be asking for stronger controls. The UK has been far more effective than any other country in creating fear.

Finance

Economists agree that we are heading for one of the worst global recessions in history. I suspect they are being optimistic and that we are heading for the worst recession in modern history. (Recessions in the 14th century tended to be very severe because the economy depended entirely upon agriculture and when the weather was bad there weren't any crops.)

In the United States the Fed is buying junk bonds, and in the UK the Bank of England has given the Government an unlimited overdraft. Capitalism has been suspended indefinitely. In 2008, the banks were bailed out with public money so that bankers didn't lose out on their bonuses. It was this recklessness waste of public money that helped launch populist governments around the world. Will the same thing happen again?

Recessions are unpleasant for everyone. Public borrowing will soar and inflation will rocket as currencies lose value. What will governments do to get rid of their debts? One option is simply to cancel all debts and to pretend they do not exist and never did exist. Another possibility is to allow inflation to erode everyone's debts. Interest rates will be kept at absurdly low levels to keep debts under control. Some governments may take the tough approach – pushing up taxes and cutting public services.

Inflation may be good for those with big debts but it can be enormously damaging to any society. What are the chances of having to take your currency to the shops in a wheelbarrow – just to pay for a loaf of bread and a couple of eggs? It is a fair bet that they are shorter than at any time in history unless you live in Germany, Zimbabwe, Venezuela or Argentina where, at various times in the last century, currencies fell far faster and further than might have seemed possible.

On 21st April, the price of West Texas Intermediate Oil fell to minus $40 a barrel. (West Texas Intermediate is a type of high quality crude oil.) Very little oil was being used around the world, and all the available storage space had been used up and so people who owned large quantities of the oil were paying others to take the stuff away and find somewhere to put it.

When the price of oil goes into negative territory, the world is in serious, serious trouble.

None of this may seem to matter to people buying petrol or diesel or home heating oil but it will matter enormously in a few months' time and it will probably matter even more in a few years' time. With such a temporary glut of oil, exploration will be dramatically reduced or will cease altogether. Climate change campaigners may cheer at this but their cheering may die away when they realise that without supplies of oil there will be no electricity to power their computers, mobile phones, electric cars or homes. (Most electricity today is, of course, still obtained from fossil fuels and as Zina Cohen explained in her book *Greta's Homework*, this will doubtless be the case for a generation or two.)

Many small businesses will go bust in the aftermath of the 'crisis', and it is difficult not to sympathise with those who suspect that this was always one of the aims of the policies executed during this manufactured 'crisis'. At the end of April 2020, the Corporate

Finance Network, which represents 12,000 accountants, estimated that 800,000 small businesses did not have enough cash to last another month. The EU has always been opposed to small companies and its agenda has always been managed by lobbyists. Similarly, big banks prefer dealing with large companies. Even though the British voted to leave the EU there seems little doubt that London will for some years follow EU attitudes and philosophies.

The one group of people who make a great deal of money out of this 'crisis' will undoubtedly be senior bankers who will doubtless find a way to make big personal profits while everyone else is suffering. No one would expect anything else. The bankers, who will wander unscathed through the chaos, will doubtless manage to demand a great deal of sympathy for themselves for the sacrifices made by their shareholders. Knighthoods and other pretty gongs will be distributed generously.

As far as personal money is concerned, the key will probably be interest rates.

As we went into the lockdown, interest rates around the world were lower than they had ever been. How long is that likely to last now? It's difficult to say but uncertainty and bad debts are likely to put pressure on all sectors of the world of finance. Central banks may want to keep interest rates low to avoid financial meltdowns but in order to attract foreign money they may need to allow them to rise. In the UK, Government borrowing will be worse than it was by the end of World War II and massively higher, as a percentage of GDP, than it was after the financial crash in 2008.

As I suggested earlier, there is a real chance that debts (governmental, corporate and private) will be forgiven in an attempt to get the economy going. The losers, of course, will be taxpayers and people who have saved rather than spent and who have no debts.

The one big certainty is that globalisation is finished.

And since it was the deflationary effects of globalisation which brought down prices, the opposite will now happen. As nationalism and protectionism become ever more popular so the prices of almost everything will rise. In a year or two even the price of oil will soar because oil companies will have pretty well stopped finding more supplies (partly because of the low price caused by the glut and partly because of pressure from environmentalists.)

In personal financial terms it is impossible to say what will happen six months ahead, let alone a year or two into the future, and so I think it is probably wise to keep debts to an absolute minimum and to try to pay off any existing loans as quickly as possible. I don't think I would want to take out a big mortgage on a house or to take on a large business loan although if a debt amnesty is introduced, doing so could clearly be a short cut to obtaining great wealth at someone else's expense.

Intergenerational conflict will mean that millennials will want more inflation (to get rid of their debts) whereas baby boomers won't want to see the value of their pensions and savings destroyed.

Jobs that seemed safe in January of 2020 may well completely disappear and that will produce much uncertainty – just adding to the already sky high levels of fear.

Finally, it seems likely that there will be a good many lawsuits as a result of the handling of the 'crisis'. Indeed, the lawsuits have already started. In late April, the American state of Missouri filed a lawsuit against the Chinese government over its handling of the original outbreak. It is not difficult to see that there will be lawsuits against other governments and their advisers.

Food

I predict that there will be widespread food shortages as broken supply chains will take a long time to mend. The absence of 'pickers' will mean that fruit and vegetables will be scarce as produce is left to rot in situ. Countries which rely on importing food will suffer most. The inevitable result will be that food prices will rise – in some areas quite dramatically. The rises will be most noticeable for fresh produce and for imported foods.

I have no doubt that in the UK, europhiles will blame the rise in food prices on our plans to leave the European Union though this will, of course, be nonsense since without having to contribute to the Common Agricultural Policy, Britain will have a huge financial advantage.

Nevertheless, these protests will be used to help reverse or water down the Brexit for which the British people twice voted.

If governments insist on repeated lockdowns and on indefinite social distancing then prices will soar even further and there will be continued shortages.

It is quite possible that, as was threatened during the first weeks of the lockdown, some form of rationing will be introduced. Informal rationing, introduced by individual supermarkets and applied to their own customers will no doubt be introduced and re-introduced from time to time as stocks of essential items run low. (Threatening to introduce rationing in order to stop panic buying was as stupid as threatening to throw petrol onto a fire to put it out but no one ever said that our politicians were over-blessed with wisdom.)

Although panic buyers were reviled before the official lockdowns began, it seems likely that panic buying will return once sales restrictions are lifted.

Since it seems extremely likely that restrictions, lockdowns and surveillance are likely to be part of our foreseeable future, it would obviously make sense for families to ensure that they have some stocks of essential items on hand. And so there will be a big demand for products such as rice and pasta which tend to have long shelf lives. Since there are also likely to be intermittent electricity shortages in future years, it would probably not be wise to purchase items which need to be stored in refrigerators or freezers. Storing items without sell by dates or best before dates (toilet rolls, soap, paper tissues and so on) may attract opprobrium from politicians and commentators but I can see no alternative. The demand for masks, disposable gloves, disinfectants and hand sanitisers will stay high.

If an expedition set off on a trip across the Arctic without enough food supplies, the leader would be castigated as reckless. Similarly, families which make no preparation for future shortages are taking chances. I suspect that the wise will endeavour to keep a three month supply of staples and basic medicines, replacing their stocks as they are used up.

The economic consequences of the 'crisis' and the supposed 'cure' for the 'crisis' could double the number of people suffering from hunger. The World Food Programme says that more than 250 million people could be affected with the risk of famine developing in Yemen and Venezuela.

Freedom

In the future, freedom is likely to be a memory rather than a reality. Those governments which took on extra powers during the 'crisis' will be very unwilling to hand back the powers they have grown to enjoy. Laws which give powers to politicians are very rarely repealed. There has been some criticism of leaders around the world (such as those in Hungary, Turkey and Russia) who have been seen to take advantage of the 'crisis' to grab more power than they had, but in truth it is difficult to think of any ruling party which hasn't built up the fear and used it to control its population more thoroughly. There is a real danger that governments which introduced tough measures (such as keeping their citizens under house arrest) on the basis they were doing so to protect the population will continue with these measures and even when the measures are withdrawn they will keep them as a threat. We will never again be as free as we were in January 2020.

Freedom of Speech

During the last two months, freedom of speech has more or less disappeared. The mainstream media all followed the Government line rather slavishly. This time it was not just the BBC which has been a disgrace. Journalists in Britain, for example, have failed to ask questions or express doubts about Government policy. Editors and journalists have behaved as though their countries were at war, and have offered their governments a level of loyalty which has been undeserved. Those writers who did try to share the truth have been subject to vicious and unfair attacks. I know this from personal experience. Everything I have written (or said) has been absolutely accurate but, as always, the truth has proved to be immensely unpopular. I have spent 50 years sharing unpopular truths on subjects such as AIDS, food and cancer, drugs, inoculation and benzodiazepines but I have never been 'monstered' or lied about as much as I have in the last couple of months. (Monstering is a term which describes what happens when a newspaper or internet site deliberately alters or adjusts or rearranges or presents the facts in order to damage the reputation of an individual.) Facts are apparently unacceptable luxuries in today's world, and those who dare to share them are likely to be demonised and regarded as unacceptably dangerous. Anyone who questions the official party line is likely to be reviled.

I do find all this worrying (and not just from a personal point of view). When I am writing or recording something, I usually check to make sure that I haven't written or said anything libellous. But when I recorded my videos about the 'crisis', I was aware that what I said might give the authorities an excuse to throw me into prison. This caution was heightened when I read that the German authorities had put a German who had complained about the lockdown into a mental hospital. (This was, of course, a procedure which was enormously widely used in the USSR.) These fears must also influence others with truths to share.

It has long been the case that anyone who writes critically about inoculation is risking serious trouble (it is, in particular, professional suicide for a doctor to say anything even remotely critical about inoculation) and writing critically about the way the 'crisis' has been dealt with has proved to be just as dangerous. In future it will be increasingly difficult to find the truth about anything because writers will be too nervous to offer any views which question the orthodox line. Freedom of speech is fast becoming a memory.

Globalisation

During the so-called 'crisis', countries learned again to be selfish. Nations within the EU acted individually rather than collectively. That will continue. The Italians and the Spanish and the Germans have all talked about the importance of preventing foreign companies taking over their industries. The French want to be more independent. The inevitable result is that the EU has no future as a federation. I predict that in the coming years, as nations struggle to escape from the coming global recession, countries all around the planet will put their own domestic needs above anything else. Globalisation is finished.

Health Care

Governments will no longer be able to afford good health care. In the UK, the NHS will be under-funded for generations. The quality of care provided by general practice, which has deteriorated massively over the last decade or two, will deteriorate still further. GPs, who have been providing advice for their patients by telephone or over the internet, may decide to limit face-to-face contact indefinitely and to carry on insisting that most consultations take place at a distance. Home visits will be even rarer than they are now. Older citizens will remember fondly the days when doctors were available 24 hours a day and 365 days a year. The deterioration of the GP service will continue to put great pressure on the ambulance service and on accident and emergency departments. Neither could cope very well before the 'crisis'. Things will deteriorate still further. At some point, private GP services will spring up in urban areas. Internet medical services will continue to expand and to provide basic medical care for millions. Ironically, the doctors providing care over the internet will be the GPs who are now working three day weeks, or on maternity leave or restricting themselves to providing telephone services for their NHS patients.

The elderly, who have already been brushed aside and denied normal human rights and freedoms, will be increasingly deprived of decent health care and encouraged to sign 'Do Not Resuscitate' forms. What the authorities don't seem to realise is that, generally speaking, the elderly suffer from less illness than individuals several decades younger than them. The over 65s tend to have 1.3 illnesses per year each, on average. The under 65s tend to have 2.1 illnesses per year each, on average. The figures prove that illness isn't the same thing as ageing.

The wisest 70 and 80-year-olds may well deny their age and insist that they are five, ten or fifteen years younger than they really are.

The pressure to accept inoculation will rise for all age groups – even to the point of compulsion.

For reasons which I do not pretend to understand, dental surgeries closed during the 'crisis'. Patients were left to treat themselves – even removing their own teeth. A number of dentists said they would not be able to reopen when the 'crisis' ended.

Home Working

During the 'crisis', millions of people were forced to work at home. Computers and the internet made it possible for people to work effectively from their spare bedroom or the dining room. Skype and Zoom have made it possible for meetings to be held without people wasting time and energy moving from one place to another. For example, magazine editorial teams discovered that it is perfectly possible to put together a magazine without any of the staff seeing one another at all. Everything can be done remotely and it doesn't matter a damn where people live.

How many people will go back to working full time in offices? How many people will go back to spending several hours a day commuting to work?

There will, of course, be some people who will be glad to get back to 'normal' office life. But there will be millions more who will have discovered that they really didn't need to go into an office at all. Or maybe they will decide that they need to meet up with colleagues, say, once a month.

The impact this will have will be enormous.

For a start, there will be less need for offices. Commercial property will slide still further in value unless and until office blocks can be converted into residential accommodation. Large businesses may find that they can rotate office accommodation, with different departments using accommodation on different days of the month. The savings will be phenomenal.

The knock on effect will also be far reaching. There will be less need for transport links and for cleaning services and so on. There will, however, be a constant need for good IT technicians to service equipment in workers' homes. And there will doubtless also be an ever growing need for courier services.

With far fewer commuters on the roads and the trains there will be far less of a need for new transport services. And with lower sales of fuel and fewer people driving into big cities, the tax take will be reduced. The air quality in cities will rise too.

Most dramatic of all, perhaps, will be the moving of many people out from suburbia and into the countryside. Those who have been locked down in small flats or tiny houses with tinier gardens will realise that if anything like this happens again (as it doubtless will) they will want to be working in the countryside and not the town. They will want more space and more garden. Working at home will make this more and more possible.

Hospitals

It seems to be generally agreed that the NHS had a good 'crisis'. NHS staff were applauded, feted and treated as heroes. I'm not so sure that the NHS did much of which it can be proud. It was, after all, NHS staff who allowed cancer patients to be denied essential treatment. NHS staff must have known that many wards were half empty and that intensive care units were nowhere near as busy as they had been before the 'crisis' began. It will take many months if not years for hospitals in Britain to catch up with the backlog of patients requiring treatment for cancer and other serious disorders. The long-term consequences will be fearful as millions of people will be aware that their own illnesses, or the illnesses of loved ones, were allowed to develop beyond treatment. And when it becomes clear that hospitals were not as busy as has been claimed and that urgent care facilities for seriously ill patients were closed down unnecessary, the affection for NHS staff may falter.

For at least six months after the lockdown has ended, hospitals will be busier than ever (far busier than they were during the false 'crisis' of March and April 2020) as an attempt is made to catch up with the backlog of patients urgently requiring attention.

Hotels, Restaurants, Pubs and Cafés

If social distancing really becomes a continuing legal requirement around the world (as has been threatened) I cannot see how any hotels, restaurants, pubs and cafés can ever open again.

For most people the whole point of dining out is to be able to share a table and eat together. If a table for four people is twelve foot square, it's going to need a lot of candles to make it romantic. And how is the waiter going to bring your food? Does he throw it to you from six feet away? Or do you leave the table while he puts down your plate and then retreats to a legally safe distance?

And what's going to happen about lifts/elevators in hotels? With a limit of two close friends per car, the queues for the lifts are going to be endless.

It is difficult to avoid the thought that the Government wants to maintain social distancing so that we are kept isolated from one another – keeping in touch only through the internet. There clearly aren't going to be many meetings or conferences or trade fairs in Britain for a long while.

Television on demand services are the big winners of the social distancing rules. Netflix signed up 16 million new subscribers in the first three months or so of 2020 – twice the number it expected.

Illness

The incidence of a wide range of illnesses will rise dramatically. The lockdown meant that people failed to exercise properly and got into bad eating habits. Many failed to get any sunshine. There will be vitamin deficiencies. Many people ate too much (and will be overweight) and many more drank too much alcohol and will be well on the way to alcoholism. (The sale of alcohol from supermarkets rose by 20% in the UK – though this probably isn't as bad as it seems since the pubs were closed, and so many people were doubtless only drinking at home what they used to drink in their favourite public house.) Many patients with symptoms of illness were unable to obtain medical help and so diseases will be far more advanced when treatment is finally provided. Unbelievably, cancer patients have been deprived of surgery and drug treatment. Mental illness will rocket during lockdown – but there will be very little help available for most sufferers. The young members of the royal family will doubtless give interviews in which they produce an endless stream of pretty obvious platitudes. I wrote the first popular book on stress in the 1970s (*Stress Control*) and I have never known a time when stress was more widespread or more damaging to both body and mind than it is at the moment.

Industry

Some industries are going to find life very different when the 'crisis' has been officially declared under control. (If that is ever allowed to happen.)

For example, the car industry has long relied on selling huge numbers of cars to fleet buyers. But this is likely to change dramatically. As more and more people work from home so there will be far less need to supply staff with vehicles. (During the lockdown period, the amount of traffic on the roads in the UK was similar to the amount of traffic commonly seen in 1955.)

On the other hand, the very same change (more people working from home) will result in an increase in the demand for light, commercial vehicles and estate cars suitable for use by delivery drivers.

And the demand will be for petrol or diesel vehicles rather than electric vehicles. No delivery driver wants a van that will only travel 100 miles without a recharge and which then needs to be left for hours before it can be used again.

Inoculation

For many years now those opposing inoculation have been under great pressure. That pressure has risen dramatically in the last year or so, and it is difficult to avoid the suspicion that there have been plans to introduce compulsory inoculations for some time. I now have a strong suspicion that governments may now be planning annual inoculations.

It is being claimed by some experts that those who catch the infection may not retain their immunity. And that they might, therefore, catch the infection a second time. Or a third time. This will, of course, mean that even people who have had the disease will need to have regular inoculations to protect them against getting the disease again.

All this, of course, is most unusual to say the least.

(To be honest, I'm not sure I believe any of this. Exposure to a specific infection usually leads to a level of immunity. People who catch an infection and survive are usually protected against future attacks. I have never known so much bollocks talked about a disease. But I know that what I believe is of little consequence.)

Flu inoculations are usually given annually because the type of flu against which the inoculation is intended to provide protection changes each year – or more often. The inoculation isn't against the same flu bug– but a different one each year. Sadly, the inoculation isn't always against whatever infection happens to be prevalent that year.

But, if it is believed that catching the 'crisis' infection doesn't provide lifelong immunity, I don't see how the much publicised proposed inoculation will provide lifelong immunity either.

And so will the authorities insist that we all have annual inoculations? Will these be against the same infection – or against a mutation?

I cannot see those inoculations being voluntary. And it would not surprise me at all if the authorities decided to put a microchip or radioactive tracer into each inoculation so that they could trace those individuals who had not had the inoculation. It seems possible that individuals who do not have the inoculation (for whatever reason) will find themselves excluded from society in many different ways – denied access to health care for example. It is also possible that a slow release drug will be introduced – ostensibly to ensure that those having the stuff from a syringe remain protected.

I wonder how many people will be made ill or killed by these inoculations. And what else will the injection do to us? What are the chances that a medicament given to the elderly might cause a lethal response?

The only certainties are that someone is going to make a hell of a lot of money out of these inoculations and it will soon be illegal to criticise inoculation programmes.

Two months ago, I would not have even thought this. But the world has changed.

Anyone who isn't paranoid isn't thinking straight.

There will, without doubt, be a rise in the number of people offering advice to those looking for a reason to be given exemption from compulsory inoculation.

It is worth noting that in the UK, preliminary work was begun in 2018 for a suitable factory to be built in Harwell, Oxfordshire.

Investments and savings

Cautious, sensible investors have lost a third or more of their savings in a few weeks. This was not, as is widely assumed, because of the 'crisis' but because of the so-called 'cure' – a 'cure' created by a succession of 'snowflake' governments which didn't know what to do except panic. It is the lockdowns all over the world which have done the damage.

Nevertheless, having some savings around is vital at a time of great uncertainty. This is a time for putting some money to one side – rather than spending it on having a good time or purchasing 'toys'. (Of course, some will feel that if we are all going to hell in a hand-basket then spending whatever they have as quickly as possible makes total sense.)

But where can we invest?

Interest rates are lower than the rate of inflation, so any money put into a bank deposit account or building society account will steadily diminish in purchasing value. Government bonds and savings accounts are utterly useless for the same reason. Property always used to be a good, safe investment but it is unlikely to be a sound investment for a good many years to come. Good jewellery, particularly gold, has always been popular at times of 'crisis' but the retail mark up on jewellery is absurdly high and makes it difficult ever to make a profit. Gold coins are probably the best type of investment, and for British investors sovereigns have the extra advantage of being officially listed as currency and, therefore, being outside the tax system. A British taxpayer can buy sovereigns and sell them at a profit without having to pay a penny in capital gains tax.

The only logical place to invest is the stock market but most investors will have sold their shares in horror and disgust when they saw prices crashing. Older investors will remember the crash of 2008, the crash of 1987 and the crash in the 1970s but it is clear that this crash really is different. Many large and well-known companies will struggle to stay alive after the lockdown. The directors of airlines, travel companies, car companies, steel companies, commercial property companies, banks and retailers are all likely to be among those who need to look up the address of a bankruptcy court.

I always eschew investments in open ended funds such as unit trusts because the costs are too high but these are now likely to be a particularly poor investment since they have traditionally been held by small investors who have a habit of panicking and selling at precisely the moment when they should be taking their courage in both hands and buying. The best answer, perhaps, is to build up a small portfolio of investment trusts which have a sound if relatively solid and unexciting investment history. Some will probably be selling at a discount and may be paying a regular, if small, dividend. This is probably not the time to put carefully collected savings into a high risk investment.

Pay

The oft-suggested idea of paying every citizen a basic salary may well become reality. Paying a simple basic salary to everyone over the age of 16 will massively simplify accounting for governments. It will mean that state benefit schemes, pensions, sick pay and so on can all be abandoned. The financial and labour savings from the simplification would be phenomenal.

Pensions

Many pensioners depend upon corporate dividends for their income. But overall dividend income will fall by two thirds this year. Indeed, there is a danger the fall will be even greater than that. And what will happen next year? Who knows? For example, banks have been 'told' by the British Government to stop paying dividends. This was cruel and typical of the uncaring and disrespectful way in which the Government has treated the elderly. The only guarantee is that directors and executives will continue to pay themselves obscene salaries and to find ways to ensure that they also receive unearned bonuses.

Some pensioners probably do not realise that they are dependent on dividends for the regular pension payments they rely on. But anyone who didn't work for the state in some way will probably receive a pension which depends to some extent on dividends. The bottom line is that pensions will either be reduced (causing great hardship now) or else pensions will be paid out of capital (causing great hardship at some point in the future). It also seems likely that state pension payments to those who have retired will be reduced and will no longer keep up with inflation.

The other effect of this reduction in dividend payments will be to reduce the power of individuals to become independent – and statist politicians will naturally be pleased by that. Statist politicians (and it seems that these days all politicians are 'statist') want everyone to be dependent upon the state.

The long-term result of the changes that are now inevitable in our society will be that workers will have to work even longer than they had planned. Indeed, the majority will probably never be able to retire – simply because their private or company pensions, when added to the state pension, will not be sufficient to live on. Only those individuals who were employed by the state in some capacity will be able to afford to become full-time pensioners. The anger at this schism will grow and grow and eventually the funds for those pensioners who worked for the state will be reduced. I don't think state employees can look forward with certainty to being able to retire as early as their predecessors.

In the years to come, it is also likely that the over 70s (and in due course the over 65s and then the over 60s) will find that they are entitled to fewer and fewer health care benefits.

There are few answers to these horrors – other than for everyone to prepare for a lifetime of work, unrelieved by a few years of retirement. Only the richest and most fortunate will be able to look forward to the traditional quiet years of gentle retirement.

Police

As the lockdown continued, the police appeared to be making up their own rules as they went along. Many seemed to completely misunderstand their role in society and to delight in finding new ways to harass those going about their lawful business. In the unlikely event that the Emergency Bill is ever repealed, the police need to be reminded that their role is to protect not persecute law abiding citizens. The Government in the UK said that citizens were allowed to shop for basic necessities but the police (and some local councils) decided that Easter eggs were not essential. Some policemen decided that cigarettes and alcohol were not essential. Some pharmacies covered up their cosmetic counters. Home owners were told off by the police for daring to go into their own gardens. Helicopters patrolled the coast to make sure that no one was swimming or sailing. The chief constable of Northamptonshire, Nick Adderley, said that if people didn't heed his warning, the police would start checking the items in shoppers' baskets and trolleys to make sure that everything being purchased was a legitimate, necessary item. He did not provide a list of legitimate, necessary items. Uniformed officers patrolled parks and used drones to look for citizens who had chosen to take their exercise in public spaces. The police wanted the right to enter private homes to see if the residents had organised a party. And, worst of all, they were encouraging members of the public to sneak on their neighbours, to tell off anyone they thought might have broken the law, or the spirit of the law, and to report repeat offenders to the authorities. It is not surprising that one retired Supreme Court Judge announced that we were living in a police state. Nor is it particularly surprising that the police let it be known that they would not be dealing with crimes such as robberies, muggings and burglaries because they were so busy making sure that members of the public were behaving themselves and not buying Easter eggs.

Despite the fact that citizens felt that they were living in a police state (where the police seem to be making up laws as they went along) there was evidence that many of those in authority felt that they were above the law.

In London, Cressida Dick, the Metropolitan police commissioner, led a demonstration of police officers which broke the law on public meetings. She and the Metropolitan police were subsequently reprimanded by the Government for flouting their own rules. It is difficult to think of a more arrogant expression of superiority though we must remember that a number of ministers, including the Prime Minister, ordered the electorate to stay put but then chose to travel to their second homes. (The Prime Minister travelled to Chequers, his official country home, for his convalescence after contracting the infection and becoming part of the 'crisis'.) Dr Catherine

Calderwood, the former Chief Medical Officer in Scotland resigned after making two trips to her second home during the lockdown period.

For the rest of us, however, the ill-defined laws were enforced with surprising vigour.

A Tesco delivery driver told me that when he found himself stuck in a police road block, he expected that when it was his turn to be questioned he would be waved through. Not a bit of it. 'What is the purpose of your journey?' he was asked by an officious officer while sitting in the cab of a large lorry filled with groceries.

The police have always preferred to take the easy solution, and tackling law abiding citizens will always be easier than tackling knife wielding criminals. It seems to me that the police have been deliberately trying to break the spirit of the people with an absurd armoury of petty rules and regulations – most of them made up by senior officers who exhibited a remarkable ignorance of the law.

The Emergency Bill has given the police massive, long-term powers which they will be reluctant to relinquish. Giving the police massive powers is like allowing a lion to taste human flesh and blood, and so the way the police have behaved should not surprise us. Researchers at Cambridge University searched and found the missing twin brothers of 13 men who were recidivists. They discovered that nine of the other 13 brothers were also recidivists and the remaining four were policemen.

Sadly, the one thing the 'crisis' has taught us is that the police cannot be trusted. They have no common sense but an uncommon sense of their own importance.

The Emergency Bill has also given council employees tough powers over the electorate. If these powers are abused (which they almost certainly will be) there will be much frustration and repressed anger.

Politics

Governments which are shown to have made large errors in the way they treated the 'crisis', will quite rightly suffer a huge failure of public sympathy and support. In order to avoid this happening, politicians will lie, lie and lie again about the seriousness of the situation and they will doubtless do everything they can to fiddle the figures to prove that they acted wisely.

The EU had a very bad 'crisis' and showed itself incapable of providing leadership. It is now much more likely that the EU will fail to survive the next five years.

China will come out of the affair very badly. Few people will now trust the Chinese, and there will be sustained anger at the way the 'crisis' is believed to have developed.

World politics is going to change. Distrust and suspicion will grow, borders will be strengthened, nationalism will be revived and globalism will become a dirty word.

Property

There are going to be many forced sellers when the 'crisis' is over. The millions of home owners who have lost their jobs will be looking to downsize or to move into rented property. Many others will be struggling with terrible debts.

Property prices in pleasant, rural areas are set to only fall a little whereas I suspect that residential property prices in urban areas will collapse by as much as a fifth or even a quarter. Top end London prices won't be much affected but I suspect that the long running London property boom might well be over. How many people will want to live in London when they can buy a lovely home in the country for the same money – and set up an office in a spare bedroom or a shed in the garden? The sale of small one room apartments may prove popular as those working from home buy a pied a terre for visits to the capital.

Once the lockdown ends, there will be a rush as buyers and sellers caught in limbo hustle to complete interrupted transactions. The over 70s, however, will remain in limbo if they are stuck in long-term or even perpetual lockdown. Their inability to move from their houses for anything other than essential shopping and a little occasional exercise will mean that they will be unable to complete or initiate property transactions. If the lockdown remains permanent for the elderly then unless they are prepared to break the law (and risk an unlimited fine) the over 70s will never, ever be able to move home even if they wish to move into smaller or sheltered accommodation.

All over the country there will probably be a demand for small, cheap lock up properties where internet sellers can store the goods they sell – and possibly use to accept mail and to pack items for mailing.

Secrecy and subterfuge

Whenever people are oppressed by what is, effectively, an occupying force, they look for (and invariably find) ways to get round the regulations.

During World War II, the French resistance managed to keep moving about in Paris even though the French capital was occupied by a ruthless army of Germans.

And if millions of over 70s are (as has been threatened) kept under house arrest in the UK until the autumn of 2021 or even 2022, then the one guarantee is that many of those people will find ways to 'escape' from their homes, to meet their families and their friends and to enjoy the autumn and early winter days of their lives.

The British Government has given courts the power to issue unlimited fines to anyone breaking free of their homes but it is difficult to see this really stopping people doing some of the things they want to do – and seeing the people who are important to them.

The Nazis were able to shoot people who disobeyed but that didn't stop some of the French moving about. I can't see British courts managing to keep people locked up more or less permanently.

All sorts of subterfuge will be used, of course. People will hide under blankets in cars and then meet in sheds and back rooms. Some may disguise themselves as delivery drivers. The over 70s will do whatever they can to make themselves look 60. Are the police really going to expect everyone to carry their birth certificates, passports, driving licences or other identifying papers with them? (It is, of course, perfectly possible that the Government will use the Emergency Bill as an excuse to introduce identity cards. However, this much hated concept will certainly result in the development of a thriving market for false papers.)

Shops

Many small and large shops will probably never open again. High streets and shopping centres will be nearly empty of shops. After weeks of house arrest, many will be cautious about shopping in busy town and city centres. The level of fear (bordering on terror) created by politicians and the media will not vanish easily.

Even charity shops will close as they struggle to deal with the probably exaggerated fear that second-hand clothing, books and so on may be infected. Health officials are likely to introduce legislation controlling second-hand clothing, books and other items, and these rules will result in the closure of many charity shops. Public libraries will either adopt new storage and sterilisation protocols or they will simply close. (I suspect that many councils will take the opportunity to close their libraries.) An enormous amount of re-useable material will end up being dumped or incinerated. Deprived of their income, many charities will demand to be supported with taxpayers' money. Politically correct charities will find themselves well supported. Fringe charities will doubtless either close or become entirely voluntary.

Shops will be under pressure to limit the number of people in a store at one time. Unhappily, I suspect that the rules about this will not be a great burden because the number of people shopping will be reduced. Millions who have become used to doing their grocery and clothes shopping online will find real world shopping too onerous.

Debts incurred during the lockdown will prove to be an impossible burden for numerous independent shop owners. Retail property values are likely to slump dramatically as large numbers of shops are put on the market – with relatively few buyers around. Shop premises are likely to remain empty for long periods as even charities stop opening new shops. Town centres are going to look like the day after the apocalypse. If new entrepreneurs buy shop premises at low prices and without historic debts, they may be able to survive but local councils will be desperate for money and will doubtless put up business rates and car park charges.

Large retailers will suffer too and those without large, well organised online shops will probably fail quite quickly. Shoppers have become accustomed to the convenience of buying online and will be reluctant to go back to the High Street – particularly when social distancing rules make shopping a tedious and time consuming nightmare. The word is that we will have to follow social distancing rules indefinitely. Standing outside, queuing to enter a shop, will cause massive congestion on often narrow pavements. And it isn't going to be much fun in the middle of winter, when there is ice on the ground and snow in the air. No one is going to go shopping for fun, browsing will be impossible and bricks and mortar shops don't have much of a future. Online shopping is going to explode and those who provide the support services (providing packaging, storage and courier services) will, like the traders who sold picks and shovels in the gold rush, probably be the people who get rich. Online shops will be expected to provide free delivery and to agree to take back items which don't fit or which are unwanted. The result will be that margins will be wafer thin.

Not even service industries will escape unscathed. Many people have learned to cut one another's hair or do their own nails. Social distancing rules will make it difficult for professional hairdressers and beauty technicians to operate successfully. And demand for their services will doubtless fall.

The only beneficiaries of all these changes will be internet companies, logistical companies and real estate companies renting out huge 'box' warehouses. Companies which have 'big box' warehouses which are well situated close to motorway junctions will probably do extremely well. However, intense competition will mean that margins in all these areas will remain low.

Smart meters

Smart meters for electricity will become compulsory. Ostensibly, this will be done to control electricity usage (which will be in short supply because of the demand for power to keep electric cars moving). In reality, it will be done to control the citizens and to check to see who is moving about too much. Those individuals who question authority will find that their electricity is turned off. Smart meters make it easy to do this from a distance. Governments will have the power to stop electric cars moving and, when self-driving cars are introduced, governments will have the power to re-direct those in any way they wish.

Citizens who wish to defy the 'house arrest' regulations will no doubt 'fool' the smart meter spies by leaving on lights even when they are out of their homes.

Sneaking and snitching

People are so riddled with senseless fear (it doesn't matter whether it was created because of a conspiracy or a cockup) that they will continue to be suspicious and distrusting of their neighbours. Bullying (whether online or in real life) will abound and there will be an increase in puritanism.

In the UK, the police have encouraged people to snitch on their neighbours. In New York, the mayor, Bill de Blasio, encouraged people to inform on those who were violating his lockdown rules. The Chinese used emergency pandemic laws to arrest 15 people in Hong Kong because they had been accused of being involved in anti-government protests.

In the end, the population will be divided into two.

On the one hand there will be the sneaks who will, bathed in self-righteousness, take great delight in dobbing in their friends, relatives and neighbours.

And on the other hand there will be those who regard sneaking as a deplorable activity.

Sadly, I fear that the sneaks will be in the majority.

Social Distancing

Is social distancing really necessary?

I don't think there is much evidence that it helps very much but it certainly causes fear, suspicion and mistrust as well as a growing sense of paranoia. It also builds up aggression and self-importance among those charged with ensuring that social distancing rules are obeyed.

The one certainty is that social distancing makes the public easier to control and to manage.

Is that just a fortunate side effect?

Social services

Neither central government nor local government will be able to afford much in the way of social services. I think we have to expect all services to be cut dramatically. And I fear that once they have been cut they will never be restored. Services to the elderly will be the first to be cut and these cuts will, I fear, be draconian.

Sporting Events

In the near future, some professional sporting events will be played behind closed doors – with television cameras providing spectators with their only chance to watch games. In the long term, sporting venues may be forced to ensure that spectators stay further apart and this will inevitably mean a dramatically reduced income. If the spectators in a football stadium have to be kept six or eight feet apart from one another then a stadium built to hold 100,000 spectators will probably only accommodate 5,000 to 10,000 safely. A season ticket will cost the price of a new medium range motorcar. Moreover, managing the flow of even such dramatically reduced crowds into and out of sporting venues will mean long delays and will further damage the popularity of sport as entertainment. Sporting events which require spectators to travel long distances will find that they are hit badly. Professional sports clubs are going to have to become accustomed to a new, far less profitable world.

(Much the same problem will be faced by musicians, of course. Having seen their record sale income slump as a result of the internet, many entertainers have chosen to tour and earn money through concerts. In the future, open air concerts will probably be more popular than concerts in closed venues but both will doubtless suffer a huge drop in income. And the success of open air concerts will depend upon the demands of the police. Ticket prices will have to rise to astronomical levels or else artistes will have to take much reduced fees.)

Amateur sports will never be as popular as they were, and team sports which require shared dressing rooms will suffer most. Golf and tennis clubs may have to reduce their charges in order to stay in business.

Status

One lesson of the 'crisis' is the widespread realisation that we have for many years under-valued the people in our society whose work is most crucial and, at the same time, we have over-valued the status of people whose work is far less important.

The status of health care workers has rocketed (even though it will eventually be clear that much of their effort has been misdirected and that by taking decisions to abandon those people who needed urgent treatment, high level health care managers may have failed to do the jobs they are paid to do) but it is now clear that the people who really matter in our daily lives are the ones who do jobs which most people always used to take for granted: the postman, the delivery driver, the supermarket checkout staff, the rubbish collectors and so on.

And the ones whose work is less important are the senior bureaucrats and administrators who are paid huge sums to shuffle bits of paper around – the ones who consider themselves far too important to do anything as demeaning as actually 'manage' or organise things. We have managed quite well without them during the 'crisis' and it is now clear that we could manage well without them pretty well indefinitely.

I hope that society finds a way to reward the hard-working, courageous folk without whom our lives would have been entirely unbearable. They need better pay not just because more money is always nice to have but because better pay means that you have been given more respect for the work you do.

So, for example, let's cut in half the salaries of the senior executives who sit in the Royal Mail boardroom. That should enable the company to damn near double the pay of the average postman and postwoman. (Sadly, I gather that Royal Mail is planning to cut back on Saturday deliveries. This will allegedly be temporary. We'll see.) And let's halve the salaries of the over-paid executives who work for our local councils, and double the salaries of the dustmen.

Taxes

For a year or so, governments will try not to raise income taxes –
and so they will introduce more hidden taxes than ever. I suspect that
tax relief on pension payments will be reduced still further and
capital gains taxes will be extended and increased. Capital gains tax
will probably be introduced for home sales. (This tax will probably
raise very little money, for it seems likely that property prices will
fall rather than rise for the foreseeable future.)

I fear, however, that these hidden taxes will not raise enough
money to pay off the massive debts which will have accumulated.

Unless debts are simply written off (a very real possibility) taxes
are going to have to rise and stay high for generations and, at the
same time, services are going to have to be cut since the extra money
raised will need to be used to pay off the interest on the debts.
Paying off the capital debts governments have incurred will take
close to forever. Inflation will soar around the world as governments
print more money to try to stay ahead of their massive debts. Interest
rates will rise too. And, until interest rates become irresistibly high,
so too will the value of gold.

In due course there is likely to be an increase in the rate of VAT,
and I can see a wealth tax being introduced. (This has been made
easier for individual governments since the International Monetary
Fund has recommended wealth taxes as a way to deal with the
consequences of the lockdowns that have been so widely
introduced.) Although wealth taxes have always done far more harm
than good and have been pretty well abandoned by most countries,
governments will be so desperate to raise money that they will
happily reintroduce taxes which seem popular to the mass of electors
and which have more of a political than an economic value. The
really rich won't pay any wealth tax, of course. The people who will
be hit will be the middle classes who don't think of themselves as
rich at all.

The one hope is that governments will use the 'crisis' as an
excuse to simplify tax regimes. In the UK, for example, the tax code
has expanded so much that not even professional tax inspectors or
tax accountants can possibly know all the regulations. The result is
that much of the nation's time is spent on preparing, finalising,
submitting and arguing over tax accounts.

Local councils will not miss the opportunity to use the 'crisis' as an excuse to put up their taxes. Commercial failures (particularly in town centres) will result in bankruptcies (with taxes being unpaid) and massively reduced footfall (with the result that car park income will drop). Tax rises will doubtless be far more dramatic than ever seen previously. And, at the same time, services will be reduced. The big financial burden on local councils has for years been servicing the pension costs of former executives. For years now local council executives have been vastly over-paid (in the UK many are paid far more than the Prime Minister). This burden will prove to be unsustainable.

For all of us, the old adage 'hope for the best, plan for the worst' seems appropriate.

Travel

Many airlines and travel companies will go bust and in future travel costs will rise dramatically. There will be pressure to cut back on international travel – particularly by flying. This will be partly a result of the realisation that there are real health risks involved in going abroad, partly a result of the fact that many business folk will realise that video conferencing really does make international travel a luxury rather than a necessity and partly a result of the fact that for a variety of reasons the cost of airline travel is going to rocket. Not many people are going to want to holiday in France or Spain when the cost of a return airline ticket has soared to $10,000. Disneyland is going to struggle to find non-local customers. Ski resorts will find life very hard.

Airlines will doubtless be ordered to reduce the number of people per plane in order to satisfy social distancing requirements but that isn't going to help very much since on many planes the air that everyone breathes is recirculated. Even on a short flight this means that everyone on board will breathe in dirty air that has been exhaled by everyone else. What this means in practice is that if there is one person on an aeroplane with an infectious disease then by the time the aeroplane lands, the chances are high that everyone on the aeroplane will have caught that disease – whatever it is.

There has been some talk of leaving the middle seat of three empty on aeroplanes but this would inevitably lead to a dramatic fall in profits or rise in the cost of airline tickets. An alternative is for airline passengers to wear masks throughout their journeys though this would mean that they would be unable to eat or drink. (Relaxing the mask rule even for a few minutes would destroy the point of wearing the masks.) It is difficult to see 12 hour flights being popular when travellers have to wear masks for the whole 12 hours – without eating or drinking anything. Travellers hoping to go to another country may need a certificate of inoculation, in the same way that travellers a few decades ago were required to have a certificate of inoculation against smallpox. Tattooed certificates may be considered more reliable, and will be welcomed by some younger folk, though politically unacceptable.

In addition, people will be constantly aware that the danger of lockdowns is ever present. Many will decide that these are not good days to plan trips abroad, whether for business or for pleasure. Do you really want to be stuck on the other side of the globe when a lockdown is announced?

Business meetings can be managed without any travel at all and most people have travelled relatively little in their own countries so there are plenty of opportunities to take holidays without having to get onto an aeroplane or travel abroad.

It isn't just aeroplanes which are best avoided, of course. Trains and buses are good places for catching bugs of one sort or another and there is, in addition, always the risk that public transport will be closed down if there is any threat of an infection. Private transport still has a future but vehicles will be used more for private reasons than for business purposes.

I suspect that, in countries all around the world, a number of tourist resorts and attractions will find that they need to concentrate on catering for customers close to home rather than attracting customers from abroad. Holiday resorts which had become unfashionable may suddenly find that they are back in favour.

It would be sensible for governments planning new infrastructure developments for travellers (new railway lines and airports) to reconsider their plans but as always where politics are concerned, the sensible route is not always the favoured route. Lobbyists will ensure that the commercial and employment advantages of expensive infrastructure projects are well promoted.

Conclusion

So that is how I see the future.

I am sorry if my thoughts seem depressing.

But it is surely better to have some idea of what may come – and to be prepared. And, of course, I could be wrong. Maybe everything will be back to normal in a month.

I suspect that we are all going to have to change our ambitions and our hopes and our plans. Life is going to become rather more like living in a science fiction novel than some might like. Those who can become at least a little independent will survive the disappointments and the frustrations of the future most easily and, dare I say it, with most self-respect and dignity. Usually, it is the young who cope best with change. But, we are going through massive, fundamental lifestyle changes and children and millennials will not cope as well as older citizens.

There is no doubt that those of us who see the truth are in a minority. There may, however, be enough dissidents to create an underground protest movement. If so, nations will be divided into those who believe their government's version of the truth and those who prefer the truth.

To paraphrase Henry David Thoreau, the mass of people are incredibly gullible and frighteningly unwilling to question what they are told – especially when they can be convinced that there is any sort of national or global 'crisis'. It is in a 'crisis' that leaders can most readily rely on the fearful following obediently. And the greater the fear becomes, the more obedient people will be.

Dear Reader
If you found this book useful I would be enormously grateful if you would post a review on Amazon or your preferred online site. It would help a great deal.
Thank you
Vernon Coleman

The Author
Biography and reference articles

Vernon Coleman was educated at Queen Mary's Grammar School in Walsall, Staffs. He then spent a year as a Community Service Volunteer in Liverpool where he was the first of Alec Dickson's 'catalysts'. (Ref 1 below). He studied medicine at Birmingham Medical School and qualified as a doctor in 1970. He has worked both in hospitals and as a GP. He resigned from the health service on a matter of principle. (Ref 2 below).

Vernon Coleman has organised many campaigns concerning iatrogenesis, drug addiction and the abuse of animals and has given evidence to committees at the House of Commons and the House of Lords. For example, he gave evidence to the *House of Lords Select Committee on Animals in Scientific Procedures* (2001-2) on Tuesday 12.2.02

Dr Coleman's campaigns have often proved successful. For example, after a 15 year campaign (which started in 1973) he eventually persuaded the British Government to introduce stricter controls governing the prescribing of benzodiazepine tranquillisers. ('Dr Vernon Coleman's articles, to which I refer with approval, raised concern about these important matters,' said the Parliamentary Secretary for Health in the House of Commons in 1988.) (Ref 3 below).

Dr Coleman has worked as a columnist for numerous national newspapers including *The Sun, The Daily Star, The Sunday Express, Sunday Correspondent* and *The People*. He once wrote three columns at the same time for national papers (he wrote them under three different names, Dr Duncan Scott in *The Sunday People*, Dr James in *The Sun* and Dr Vernon Coleman in the *Daily Star*). At the same time he was also writing weekly columns for the *Evening Times* in Glasgow and for the *Sunday Scot*. His syndicated columns have appeared in over 50 regional newspapers in the United Kingdom and his columns and articles have appeared in newspapers and magazines around the world. Dr Coleman resigned from *The People* in 2003 when the editor refused to print a column criticising the Government's decision to start the Iraq War. (Ref 6 below)

He has contributed articles and stories to hundreds of other publications including *The Sunday Times, Observer, Guardian, Daily Telegraph, Sunday Telegraph, Daily Express, Daily Mail, Mail on Sunday, Daily Mirror, Sunday Mirror, Punch, Woman, Woman's Own, The Lady, Spectator* and *British Medical Journal.* He was the founding editor of the *British Clinical Journal.* For many years he wrote a monthly newsletter called *Dr Vernon Coleman's Health Letter.* He has worked with the Open University in the UK and has lectured doctors and nurses on a variety of medical matters.

Vernon Coleman has presented numerous programmes on television and radio and was the original breakfast television doctor on TV AM. He was television's first agony uncle (on BBC1's *The Afternoon Show*) and presented three TV series based on his bestselling book *Bodypower.* In the 1980s, he helped write the algorithms for the first computerised health programmes – which sold around the world to those far-sighted individuals who had bought the world's first home computers. (Ref 4 below). His books have been published in the UK *by Arrow, Pan, Penguin, Corgi, Mandarin, Star, Piatkus, RKP, Thames and Hudson, Sidgwick and Jackson, Macmillan* and many other leading publishing houses and translated into 25 languages. English language versions sell in the USA, Australia, Canada and South Africa as well as the UK. Several of his books have appeared on both the *Sunday Times* and *Bookseller* bestseller lists.

Altogether, he has written over 100 books which have, together, sold over two million copies in the UK alone. His self-published novel, *Mrs Caldicot's Cabbage War* has been turned into an award winning film (starring Pauline Collins, John Alderton and Peter Capaldi) and the book is, like many of his other novels, available in an audio version.

Vernon Coleman has co-written five books with his wife, Donna Antoinette Coleman and has, in addition, written numerous articles (and books) under a vast variety of pennames (many of which he has now forgotten). Donna Antoinette Coleman is a talented oil painter who specialises in landscapes. Her books include, *My Quirky Cotswold Garden.* She is a Fellow of the Royal Society of Arts. Vernon and Antoinette Coleman have been married for more than 20 years.

Vernon Coleman has received numerous awards and was for some time a Professor of Holistic Medical Sciences at the Open International University based in Sri Lanka.

Reference Articles referring to Vernon Coleman
Ref 1
'Volunteer for Kirkby' – *The Guardian,* 14.5.1965
(Article re VC's work in Kirkby, Liverpool as a Community Service Volunteer in 1964-5)
Ref 2
'Bumbledom forced me to leave the NHS' – *Pulse*, 28.11.1981
(Vernon Coleman resigns as a GP after refusing to disclose confidential information on sick note forms)
Ref 3
'I'm Addicted To The Star' – *The Star*, *10.3.1988*
Ref 4
'Medicine Becomes Computerised: Plug In Your Doctor.' – *The Times*, 29.3.1983
Ref 5
'Computer aided decision making in medicine' – *British Medical Journal*, 8.9.1984 and 27.10.1984
Ref 6
'Conscientious Objectors' – *Financial Times magazine,* 9.8.2003

Major interviews with Vernon Coleman include
'Doctor with the Common Touch.' – *Birmingham Post*, 9.10.1984
'Sacred Cows Beware: Vernon Coleman publishing again.' – *The Scotsman*, 6.12.1984
'Our Doctor Coleman Is Mustard' – *The Sun,* 29.6.1988
'Reading the mind between the lines.' – *BMA News Review,* November 1991
Doctors' Firsts – *BMA News Review,* 21.2.1996
'The big league of self publishing.' – *Daily Telegraph,* 17.8.1996
'Doctoring the books' – *Independent,* 16.3.1999
'Sick Practices' – *Ode Magazine,* July/August 2003
'You have been warned, Mr Blair.' – *Spectator,* 6.3.2004 and 20.3.2004

'Food for thought with a real live Maverick.' – *Western Daily Press,* 5.9.2006
'The doctor will see you now' – *Independent,* 14.5.2008

There is a more comprehensive list of reference articles on www.vernoncoleman.com

Printed in Great Britain
by Amazon

48213593R00078